THE BEER KITCHEN

By Melissa Cole

hardie grant books

**The art & science of cooking,
& pairing, with beer**

For Granddad

From walking me around your 'estate' (aka the back garden veg patch) to check on the progress of this year's crop to giving my first memorable sip of nutty ale, you were fundamental in forming my beer and food journey and I wish you were here to see this published; I miss you still.

Contents

'Never underestimate how much assistance,
how much satisfaction, how much comfort, how
much soul and transcendence there might
be in a well-made taco and a cold bottle of beer.'

Tom Robbins, *Jitterbug Perfume*

Before you start

Please read theses notes before you
make a start on the recipes.

Notes on the recipes

Use one set of measurements.

1 teaspoon = 5 ml.
1 tablespoon = 15 ml.
1 cup = 250 ml.

Fruit, vegetables and eggs are medium sized, unless otherwise stated.

Use fresh ingredients, including herbs and spices, unless otherwise stated.

Cooking instructions give conventional oven temperatures, so if you have a fan oven, the recommendation is that you decrease the temperatures given by 20°C (40°F). However, all ovens are different – my oven, for example, runs hot by 20°C (40°F), which makes a real difference to low and slow stuff. So I strongly recommend you buy an oven thermometer as they are much more accurate.

Measurements of beer in the recipes are given in grams rather than millilitres when they need to be absolutely accurate (see page 27).

I mostly use neutral oils in my cooking but a basic olive oil is fine for everything except high-temperature cooking; save the high-quality oils for dressings.

I have absolutely no financial (or other) arrangement to include any of the equipment, food or beer brands; I'm just speaking as I find.

Each main-course recipe has some suggestions of beers to cook with and also to pair with, although, as always, feel free to experiment and find your own favourites.

Why Beer & Food?

My cooking with beer campaign started
in earnest about 10 years ago, when I was
looking at what appeared, initially, like a
tasty-sounding recipe for a steak and ale pie,
but when I read it, the recipe called
for 'beer'…

That was it, just beer.

Not a hint was given whether you should use a lager or an ale, let alone specifying a bock or a bitter, a kölsch or a mild, and this confused me because I knew, even then, that the use of different beer styles would have a fundamental impact on the end dish.

And then I got annoyed because as I turned the pages of the magazine, I read more recipes, some using wine and, often, in those ones the writers were being *really* specific about which variety.

So I started scanning the pages of other food magazines I had and, at the very least, the recipe creators cared enough to say 'full-bodied red' or 'fruity, dry white' and, 'if you wouldn't drink it, don't cook with it' – but when it came to beer there was this big blind spot that 'any old beer will do' – naturally, I disagreed quite strongly then and even more vehemently now.

Your choice of beer is bigger than ever and using 'any old beer' in recipes is rarely going to end well for either you or the beer and could well put you off for life – which would be sad, because beer is ace and cooking with it can yield fabulous results – so that's why I've written this book! HOWEVER, I have a little confession to make before I go any further and it's this: a lot of my cooking with beer experiments have resulted in some disgusting crimes against food – phew, it feels good to get that off my chest – and the point behind telling you this is that I've made the mistakes, so you don't have to. Seriously, along the way I have managed to repulse any number of friends and family members with the results – one of the worst mistakes being an American-style double IPA chicken stew that tasted like mouldy grapefruit and burning rubber tyres (don't do this kids – seriously, it's horrible).

But, after quite a few of these inedible dinners and subsequent take-away orders, I decided to take a more scientific approach to the process and set myself a series of questions. How does temperature play a role? Where in the dish would that beer have the most impact? Why is there an unpleasant flavour when I do this, that or the other? What seems to always work well and why?

And thanks to the bravery of family and friends, who continued being my guinea pigs (particularly the long-suffering Mr Melissa), patterns slowly became clear and, as theories on what was happening with various beer styles when they were used in different ways were formed, they have been tested rigorously over and over again in various ways. This is the result.

Truth Time

So, truth time. Hopefully you won't run away. Some of these recipes are quite wordy, some don't follow 'conventional wisdom' and some of them tell you things take quite some time. That's because I won't lie to you.

I won't, for example, pretend that you can properly caramelise onions in 5 minutes; you can't. You can cook them light brown with slightly burnt edges, but in that time you cannot get them to that lovely, slippery, sweet state that is such unctuous bliss – it's physically impossible.

I also won't say to you that a lot of these dishes don't take some effort to make, although quite a few of them don't. And I can promise they have all been rigorously tested by, or on, friends and family. Even my Dad – whose culinary prowess normally extends to tomato soup and grated cheese sandwiches or (an admittedly perfect) dippy egg and soldiers – has tested some of these out and not poisoned anyone (yet).

There will be lots of things that you might question because it's normal advice turned on its head but there's a strong, normally scientific, rationale for everything and a lot of the time it's because I've spent hours reading papers online and thumbing through the tremendous contributions to food science in the work of people like Harold McGee, Michael Ruhlman, Heston Blumenthal, Michael Pollan, Samin Nosrat and J. Kenji López-Alt. And I have to give a massive nod to the brilliant concept of multiple recipe testing and amalgamation of the best bits by Felicity Cloake.

And I don't just use beer because I'm obsessive about it; I use beer where it makes a dish better. If it hasn't improved the dish then I haven't included the recipe because, first and foremost, I really want you to make tasty food.

Also, there may be beers you've never heard of; that's ok, don't panic, that's what the experts at your local bottle shop, online beer forums or internet searches are for. Or you can come and ask me on social media, I'm pretty chatty... (stop laughing, those of you who know me!).

Finally, my fondest hope is that you'll share this food and beer journey with friends and family because, just as I believe that beer is first and foremost a social lubricant, food is a temporary social glue, drawing people together for a few hours around a table to enjoy precious time with one another before the real world rudely intrudes... and all I want to do is help you stave that off, even if it's just for a little while.

How Beer is Made

So, how's beer made? Well, like most things in life, there's a simple answer, and a complicated explanation.

This is the simplest way to make beer.

First you need malted grains – this is mainly barley that has been fooled into thinking it's springtime and started to germinate. You then arrest that growth and toast them to a greater or lesser degree to get everything from a pale gold colour to deepest black.

You then take those grains, and steep them in hot water, allowing them to rest there for a while. This allows the starches in the grains to turn into sugar through clever enzymes.

Once this has happened, around 60–90 minutes later, you run more hot water over the top and wash those sugars through, to create a sweet liquid called the wort, which you filter into another vessel called the copper.

Copper is short for copper kettle and that is exactly what it is; it's a blooming great version of the kettle you have at home.

So, you boil up the sweet wort and then this is where you add hops, these are the plants that add flavour, bitterness and aroma to beer and that also have natural anti-microbial properties.

You then cool your hopped wort and add the magic ingredient, yeast. Yeast converts the sugars into carbon dioxide and alcohol and that, ladies and gentlemen, is how to make beer… simple huh?

Well, as I said at the beginning, there is a simple answer and a complicated explanation to everything in life and that is the simple answer.

The explanation is significantly more complicated, and perhaps here isn't the place to do that, and I may as well take the opportunity to take you back to my previous two books: *Let Me Tell You About Beer* and *The Little Book of Craft Beer* for more information. Now, on with some more 'personal' science!

The Science Bits

So, you saw the word 'science' on the cover of this book and still bought it? Brilliant. But I have a confession to make: I'm not a scientist. I don't have a scientific qualification to my name.

But, before you slam the book closed and write an angry online review, I want to let you know that what I *am* is a good journalist and I'm also *really* nosy and I don't let up. I pull threads to find facts and I weave strands of interesting relevant statements into each other and research voraciously until stories come together that fascinate me and, hopefully, other people.

If you doubt that I'm always curious about everything, if you ever meet my big sister Melanie, and ask her what my favourite word was from the time I could talk, she will roll her eyes heartily and say, in resigned and weary tones, 'why?'.

Anyway, torturing my extremely loving and tolerant sister aside, the whole subject of beer has fascinated me for nearly two decades, and my obsession with cooking followed shortly afterwards, which means I have a lot of those facts, statements and research articles at my disposal and they have all led to this point.

So, yes, I am going to hit you with a fair whack of science in this book; it's not because I'm showing off (which I do from time to time) or because I want to seem smarter than you (I'm probably not), it's because I want to tell you a story about a dish or a pairing, I want you to understand its narrative – some of which will come from the soul and some from the science – and how I arrived at the final version.

All that said, my main job is to be a conduit to disseminate information, and I think one of the most important bits of information I can give you before we get into all the recipe bits is about how your perception of taste and flavour works.

The Story *of* Taste and Flavour

There is a distinct, and important, difference between taste and flavour.

Taste is prosaic. It is an evolutionary by-product of our need to detect nutrients and toxins and, as such, is the biological analysis of food and non-food items that are put in your mouth. These are currently broken down into 5 distinct qualities: sweet, sour, salty, bitter and umami.

Just in case you aren't familiar with the last one, umami was first coined as a separate taste in 1908 by Kikunae Ikeda of Tokyo Imperial University, when he was researching the strong and delicious flavour in seaweed broth (he also then went on to develop monosodium glutamate or MSG), and while it was widely acknowledged in Eastern cuisine and scientific circles for a century or so, it was a study done at Oxford in 2000 that confirmed its status as the fifth flavour on the world stage.

Umami is all about the mouth-watering perception of savoury, and is found in in aged meats, cheeses like Parmesan, seaweed, soy and lots of items that are based on aged yeast like Marmite and, as a result, can be found in well-aged beers as well.

There are several compounds that trigger umami taste receptors and include glutamate, a salt of glutamic acid, specific ribonucleotides, and glutamate salts including monosodium glutamate (MSG), potassium glutamate and calcium glutamate. MSG has been heavily stigmatised as producing headaches, although there is no verifiable scientific study that proves this is the case, and any 'cotton mouth' you get is more likely to come from the high salt content in lots of takeaway meals.

It wouldn't surprise me at all if, in the very near future, fat were added to these definitions of taste. Growing scientific weight is being given to the fact that fat fulfils all the criteria of being a taste, and there could be others joining it too, like kokumi, which is a sensation of 'heartiness'.

Flavour on the other hand, is the result of an array of multi-sensory inputs and volatile chemical reactions, starting with how things look – which multiple studies have shown is an important part of flavour perception – and including temperature, texture, how much pain it may cause and, of course, how it smells and tastes. All these things play an important part in how we perceive what we put in our mouths.

The subject of 'mouthfeel' is an important one, and in tasting terms is broken down into two distinct areas: there are the chemical reactions, called trigeminal, and then there are the textural aspects, called tactile. Research by scientists at the University of Queensland in early 2018 has

opened a lot of doors to this 'last frontier', as it's probably the most under-researched element of gustatory pleasure. They've discovered that tongue tactility has a huge role to play in why people don't like certain foods; a good example being, why one person's love of oysters is another person's idea of slurping snot. (I'm firmly in the first camp by the way, but it doesn't matter if you're not.)

Environment has a role to play as well. Did you know, for example, that sound can have a fundamental effect on your sense of taste? Very simplistically, lower frequencies can amplify saltiness and bitterness, while higher frequencies amplify sweetness – if you want to know more then look up Professor Charles Spence's work in the area, it's fascinating.

A really good example of mistaken attribution of environmental factors in how we perceive flavours and tastes is best exemplified by plane food, which we all know is utter rubbish, right?

Well, ok, it's not exactly haute cuisine, but what we all know is, in fact, somewhat unfair. Everything from the altitude to the lack of humidity in a plane has a horrifying effect on our sense of taste and flavour but it's also been shown that a huge part of palate suppression during a flight is also due to the dull roar of the jet engines and that can also explain why what you eat in a raucous pub or restaurant is very often unmemorable (yeah, blame it on that, not the five pints you had – I'm planning to). So, maybe something else to think about when you're setting the table should be is that thrash metal really what you want? Or is there maybe a better soundtrack to complement your dinner?

And, finally, if you've managed to stick with me through all that, then here's perhaps the most important piece of scientific information I can give you: everyone's palate is individual.

You see, while I am really keen on the science aspect of taste and flavour, it is an inexact one because we are inexact beings. As Gordon M. Shepherd succinctly puts it in his book *Neurogastronomy*: 'A common misconception is that foods contain the flavours. Foods do contain the flavour *molecules* but *flavours* of those molecules are actually created by our brains.'

It's easy to understand this because we all know that our brains are unique and this means you will taste things differently to the way I do, you will enjoy things I don't, I will love things you hate but, as a general rule, we will agree on more than we differ.

How to Assess a Beer

One of the things I am most often told by enthusiastic imbibers is: 'I could do your job', and they might be right but it's mine and I'm keeping it!

I'm obviously doing myself down there, because I've put in a lot of hard yards to get to where I am, and my knowledge and skillset is strong in this arena, which is why I judge at competitions the world over. But it doesn't take a lot of work to become a better beer taster, which is a very transferable skill to other drinks or culinary arts.

The first thing to understand is: the nose knows.

Roughly 80 per cent of what we get as aromas will also be what we interpret into flavours. You can't, for example, smell how bitter a beer might be – which will always be a key component in beer in some way, shape or form, even if it's a lack of it – but you can smell everything from coffee to turpentine and cat's pee to candy canes, and all of those things have associations that your brain makes a leap on.

The best way to initially assess a beer is with short, sharp 'bunny' sniffs. This allows for any strong odours to be approached cautiously, to give your nose time to adjust to the dominant aromas, and then, later, you can inhale more deeply to further examine the more subtle, nuanced smells.

Secondly, you want to take a reasonable gulp and swish it about your mouth. This gives not only your tongue – which is your primary flavour and taste-sensing unit – the chance to get as much information as possible, but it also hits the other clusters of taste buds and sensory equipment around your mouth, allowing for the maximum transmission of information to your brain.

There are four pertinent types of physical feedback mechanisms on your tongue and they are called filiform, foliate, fungiform and circumvallate papillae.

One

Filiform are all about texture. Filiform are the 'roughness' of your tongue and deal in the texture or 'feel' of things. They don't have any correlation to taste or flavour.

Two

Foliate are ridge-shaped and are found more at the sides of the tongue and these receptors have an extra sensitivity for sourness.

Three

Fungiform are the workhorses of the tasting papillae. They are all-rounders when it comes to the perception of the five flavours.

Four

Circumvallates hang out at the back of the tongue and have an extra sensitivity to bitterness – almost certainly an evolutionary last line of taste defence against swallowing something poisonous.

Intensity of Flavour

Your first stop when you're thinking about how to pair beer with food. How intense is this beer? Is it like a fairy sprinkling dust on your taste buds, or is it like a giant taking a sledgehammer to them? Or somewhere in between? Because you need to think about that when you're pairing your dishes. There needs to be a balance of strength or one will overwhelm the other, meaning it's not a partnership, it's a war in your mouth.

For me, the single most important factor when assessing beer for a pairing is its relative bitter/sweet/acidic balance and how that compares to your dish – and it's why it's absolutely vital for you to get to know your beer before you start thinking about pairing it with food.

So, let's start with the most divisive flavour in beer: bitterness.

Begin with Bitterness

Bitterness is generally nature's way of saying 'stay away' – it's like the brightly coloured dart frog in the Amazonian rainforest or the rattle of a snake in the tall grass. When we were first hunter-gathering, it told our tongue, in no uncertain terms, to inform our brain to stay away.

But, over time, it also told us there might be some nutritional value there, as in bitter foods like broccoli or the dreaded Brussels sprout (I love them by the way, which may also explain why I like bitter beers so much).

It might interest you to know that there are more genetic markers for bitterness than for any other taste and that there are bitterness receptors throughout the body, in the lungs, nose, gut and brain; why remains a relative mystery, but it would seem it's something to do with keeping ourselves healthy. I'm pretty sure these receptors are what tell me after weekends at beer festivals, not known for their healthy food offerings, to have a few days of water and green vegetables.

It can also be the most intense aspect of a beer and is probably the largest factor you need to be aware of, not only in pairing with dishes, but when cooking with beer too (see Cooking with Beer, page 24). The bitterness in beer comes, primarily, from when the alpha acids in hop resins (see Fig.1, below) are boiled during brewing and undergo a transformative process called isomerisation to produce iso-alpha acids, which are intensely bitter.

Fig. 1

Overly bitter beer pairings have been responsible for spoiling my enjoyment of a meal more times than any other aspect of a beer. As Gwen Conley and Julia Herz point out in their book, *Beer Pairing: the Essential Guide from the Pairing Pros*, that bitter 'green' flavour in hops can clash horribly with dishes, especially where there's already even the smallest bitter elements present. This can overwhelm every other aspect of a dish and it's why that assessment of the intensity of bitterness is so very important, and just one of the reasons why I say 'get to know your beer'.

However, all those big red warning flags aside, sometimes bitterness can

be the perfect foil for certain dishes such as a slow-roast ox cheek with celeriac mash. Instead of putting bitter greens on the plate, maybe have some sweet peas and get that bitter 'cut through' from a grassy, piney American-style red ale instead.

It's also important to understand that bitterness doesn't just come from hops either, it can also come from darker malts and adjuncts like coffee (adjuncts are ingredients that are outside the base four of water, malted barley, yeast and hops) and can work in intensifying concert on the palate with astringency, which comes from tannins present in both these sources.

A final thing to watch out for is that it is widely held (but still to be fully scientifically confirmed) that the bittering compounds in beer can, in concert with the primary irritants of ethanol (alcohol) and carbon dioxide (fizz), exacerbate the effect of the painful compound in chilli (capsaicin) on the tongue, so any relief you feel reaching for a big IPA with your spicy food will only be a temporary salve from the low temperature and will end up being the opposite of a cure. To put it more simply, if you want to eat food that melts your face, unless you're a bit of a masochist, you're probably better off with a milkshake.

Beer Styles

These are the most versatile, forgiving and easy-to-use styles of beer to keep on hand. Keep a couple of bottles of each in a cool, dark place and you'll be able to use them in not just my recipes, but plenty of your own (and please contact me on social media with your work, I love seeing other people's success when cooking with beer). I have also suggested some of my favourite food and beer pairing combinations for most of the recipes.

Just one word of caution and this is not a beer snobbery thing, it's a genuine warning. Try to stay away from commodity brands and anything in green or clear bottles, with the exception of wild and mixed fermentation beers as they don't need to protect hop aroma as a general rule. A lot of the commodity brands use a pure hop bitterness extract, which reacts in unpredictable ways when cooking, more often than not producing an overtly, and unpleasant, bitter finish. Also a lot of them have a characteristic called light strike, which results from a breakdown of hop compounds because neither clear nor green glass protects them from UVA/UVB damage, that will leave an odd dusty/rubbery note to your dish.

Most Used

Belgian-style wheat beer:
a sweetish, very low bitterness, creamy citrus beer that has orange peel and coriander seeds in it

German-style hefeweizen:
a cloudy wheat beer, very low bitterness, with everything from banana & bubbelgum to clove and tomato vine notes in it

German-style dunkelweizen:
low bitterness with chocolate and banana notes

Traditional saison:
dry, medium low bitterness with an earthy pepperiness

Flanders-style red:
low bitterness, tart, dry, fruity and oaky

British-style mild:
literally meaning mildly-hopped, will generally be a dark, low ABV beer but do check

Milk stout:
can vary in strength but generally medium bitterness with a creaminess from the unfermentable lactose (milk sugar) used in it

Imperial stout:
a medium-high, strong alcohol beer with coffee, chocolate and often has fruity/floral note

Good to Have

UK-style strong ale:
encompassing the categories of Scotch ales, barley wine and old ale, generally fruity and boozy

Gose (can be subtly fruited):
lightly salted, directly sour and often fruited, generally quite low ABV, negligible bitterness

Berliner weisse (can be fruited):
directly sour and often fruited, generally quite low ABV, negligible bitterness

Fruit beer:
base style varies, often wheat or sour but this really is one to do your homework on, depending on your preferences

Fruited lambic:
dry, complex, earthy and generally berry fruit flavours (but not always), very low bitterness.

Lambic-style:
earthy, dry, complex sourness and very low bitterness

American-style pale ale:
grapefruit, rose/geranium/orange peel, with a medium-high bitterness

New Zealand-hopped pale ale/saison: floral, vinous and lightly earthy

Cooking with Beer

These are my personal golden rules when cooking with beer, which have stood me in good stead.

Do

<u>Do</u> use beers as a seasoning – just as brewers use hops as a seasoning, so can you. Want to add a herbal note to a dish, how about a classic British bitter? Want to add some lush tropical notes to a simple cheesecake? Add some Australian-style pale ale. Want to play with sweet vinous notes in a chicken casserole? Why not pop a New Zealand-hopped saison in there? And it can go on and on.

<u>Do</u> taste as you go – one of the best things you can do is test your food as you cook (avoiding dangerous raw products of course!).

<u>Do</u> think of acidity – acidity is as much a flavour intensifier as salt is. You might not need that added salt, in fact it might be counter-productive. What you might need is a dash of Berliner weisse instead.

<u>Do</u> leave the room and come back in again before you serve your food – you will get so much more pleasure from the food you've worked hard to cook if your senses aren't saturated with it. You can just stick your head out the window or into a pot of scented body lotion or the like, that'll do the trick too – ok, that's not strictly a beer-related tip, it applies to all cooking but it's a really good bit of advice, so I thought I'd sneak it in!

Don't

Don't deglaze your pan with beer – all this does is burn the sugars in the beer, which creates bitter compounds, concentrates hop bitterness and drives off all the aroma compounds.

Don't use perceptually bitter beers in dishes that cook at high heat or for more than 10 minutes – all you're doing is reducing them down to a bitter mess.

Don't be scared to use blends – if you look at the Venison Beerguignon recipe on pages 166–167 you'll see that I've used different beers for their different qualities, one is adding richness, some are adding fruitiness and another is adding bright acidity to the end of the dish – it's all about being strategic about where you add them in the dish.

Don't just think about adding beer, think about how it will enhance the flavours – what does it actually add to the dish should always be your first question, if it's basically nothing then save it for your mouth, not the pot.

Cooking with Beer
Random Advice

Be prepared: There's a reason why chefs talk about their 'mis' or mis en place – it's the preparation that allows them to work clean, smart and quick. Read your recipe, make sure you've got everything and in the correct amounts (I regularly forget that I need to halve a recipe and end up cooking for the 5,000 … hello freezer!) and get your prep done in advance so you can focus on the method. It's where, for me, plastic tubs and ramekins (custard cups) come in. I weigh out everything and put it in order of use; this also helps me know where I am in a recipe if (or inevitably when) I get distracted.

Try and keep your surfaces clear: Due to my uncontrollable kitchen gadget purchasing habit this is a constant battle for me but I've come up with a few cunning tricks over the years.

– Where possible, buy utensils with loops on them, then attach hooks with strong suckers or those non-damaging removable ones to your kitchen tiles and hang them from those. It's easier to grab them than from a tangled utensils pot and means you don't have to drill into your tiles.

– Also use these hooks with a bit of looped butcher's twine through the centre of the rolls to put your paper towel, foil, baking parchment and vacpac bags within easy reach. It doesn't work with cling film (plastic wrap), but if you buy the one in the easy-cut dispenser boxes you'll never get those maddening mangled lumps of the stuff again!

– A stick-on magnetic knife rack makes it easy to grab knives in a hurry, will keep them safer from blunting than in a drawer and doesn't take up space on a surface like a knife rack.

– Shelf 'steps' allow you to see pots and jars of things more clearly.

– Use drawer organisers for cutlery and other bits.

– The tops of your kitchen cabinets are good homes for unwieldy or rarely used bits and bobs.

Chopping: One of the things I was taught, whilst working with a chef, is how to hold a knife properly when doing a lot of chopping, particularly if you want precise control over what you're doing. It sounds scary, but it's not. All you do is move your thumb and first two fingers to grip down from the handle to hold the deepest part of the blade. It's not only more effective, it's far more comfortable if you're doing a lot of prep (see Fig. 2).

Keep a bowl on hand for trimmings: I'm not the cleanest of cooks; I keep promising myself that I'll be more ordered and methodical when I'm not working but I have an odd switch in my brain that drives my other half mad. If I'm cooking 'professionally' I am ordered, methodical, tidy, work clean and wash up after myself. If I'm cooking for 'fun', I'm more akin to a nightmare whirlwind. In fact, early experiments resulted in me getting the nickname 'The Atomic Chef' given to me by a former university housemate's dad when he walked in on a croquette-making experiment that made the kitchen look like an explosion in a flour factory; it was also the first time I cooked for my other half very early in our relationship… he's either a very patient, or a very foolish man, can never decide.

Plan your shops: This is my biggest failing. I get so easily distracted in markets and stores when I'm shopping that I frequently forget to pick up what I went in for and will walk away with edible flowers, exotic spices and pig cheeks but not the milk.

So, be less me, plan your shop, use online delivery services and, if you're busy, check online for more unusual ingredients before spending a whole Saturday trawling through specialist shops.

That said though, befriend any local businesses you can and, if you have the luxury of a bit of time, do support them. I use my local butcher, greengrocer, bottle shop and fishmonger a lot, but then I work for myself and can walk, hop on my bike or get a bus to them, but if you ring and put in an order to pick up at the weekend then you'll be putting money back into your local community and building a handy relationship for when you want unusual things like pig's trotters or cod's roe.

Cooking with Beer
Random Advice

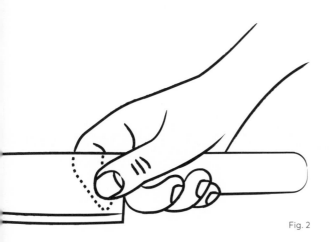

Fig. 2

Use your freezer: I would say it's a rare day when I don't reach into my freezer for something or another and it also helps me be less wasteful with food too.

Bits and bobs of beers go in the freezer all the time. I have generic beer pots on the go of porters/stouts or bitters, ESBs, barley wines, a wheat beer pot or one for sweeter beers or sour beers for chucking into various dishes to liven them up a bit and I put those in the little sauce pots you get with takeaways (yes, I eat takeout food, I am not a saint and I am also frequently knackered or getting home too late to cook).

Things to think about: apple turning a bit soft? Core, peel, chop and freeze to make apple sauce with a splash of Belgian wheat beer the next time you are grilling a pork chop or, maybe a bit healthier, pop it in a juice. Banana going too brown? Peel it and put it in the freezer for a smoothie, to mush onto toast or pancakes or make banana bread… I think you're getting the picture here.

Also good to freeze are egg wash, whites or yolks from recipes that call for one part or the other; breadcrumbs made from stale bread and obviously making big batches of things like My Mum's Spag Bol (page 67) means freezing in individual portions, or whatever's right for your household, and means a nutritious meal is on hand at the drop of a hat.

There is a lot to be said too for keeping some frozen fruits and vegetables in your freezer. It means you can make a simple tasty dinner at a moment's notice. Fry some frozen chopped onion, garlic and ginger (your own or shop bought) in a little oil until soft, then add some frozen spinach pellets, spices, tinned chickpeas (garbanzos) and a tin of tomatoes, simmer for 20 minutes and serve with rice or pasta. Replace the chickpeas with some frozen prawns (shrimp), add some wheat beer, reheat a frozen Flexible Flatbread (page 50) that's been lightly brushed with some water and you've upgraded to a fancy tasty dinner without turning a hair.

Also, keep your vegetable trimmings or veg that's past its best (assuming they aren't manky of course!) and the next time you want to make the Beer-poached Chicken (page 70) or some stock from something else you don't have to spend on fresh veg. You'd be amazed how quickly you can accrue enough to make stock. The tough outside layer of skin of the fennel bulb and onion from the Porchetta (page 172) can go in, as can the little roots that you trim off garlic cloves. Carrot peelings from washed carrots, trimmed ends of celery, tough sticks or the strings can all go in. Basically, anything that could be used in a stock that isn't going to give it a starchy or boiled veg water flavour (bitter green or starchy veg mostly), you can save in a pot in the freezer – meaning you can knock up a thrifty and tasty stock in a heartbeat – bonus.

And remember I told you that while my freezer is a busy place, it's not a giant chest freezer, just an ordinary fridge freezer with four drawers. My secret weapon to having enough space and keeping it all in order is my vacpac machine and a permanent marker. Trust me when I say write on your frozen food containers – labels fall off and your memory is rarely as good as you think it will be!

One last note

Just before you get stuck in, I want to mention an anomaly you might notice in some of the recipes, in that sometimes I'll use grams and sometimes I'll use millilitres for measurements of beer.

There's a good reason for this. Different liquids have different densities and where I need to be absolutely accurate because it's something like, say, a brine, then I will always use grams not millilitres because brines are measured by weight not volume.

However, where it's something that is more forgiving, like a sauce or something like that, I will use millilitres because it's not so important to be absolutely accurate and, after all, I am just a home cook who happens to have a bit of a speciality, not a professionally trained chef.

And, just before you go, one more quick thing. I hope you enjoy cooking from this book and the pairings that go with the recipes. But my biggest wish is merely a springboard to a lifetime of creativity with beer amongst your family and friends.

Sweet Like Chocolate

and brioche and caramel and toffee and ...

Sweetness in Beer ...

Beer, in its base form, is a naturally sweet product. As discussed in How Beer is Made (page 11), the sugary wort is fed to the yeast to eat and, without the balance of hops or other bittering or souring agents, beer would be halfway to Ovaltine (if it ever got there without being infected by wild yeast and bacteria, that is, which is highly unlikely).

The interplay of a number of factors affects the perceptual levels of sweetness in beer and can be very important when pairing – and even more so when cooking – with beer.

I'm also going to stop here to have a little rant. Apologies but I feel it has to be said. There has been a recent trend towards telling people how many International Bittering Units (IBUs) there are in a beer, which drives me insane. IBUs are a brewer's tool; they are there as a guideline for their recipes and offer the average drinker, who has no idea what on earth it means, another reason to be put off beer because it seems so bewildering.

Then there's another layer. There's the people who talk about IBUs as though they are the holy grail; like this is the only thing that could possibly make a beer great. They can put people off beer entirely because this sort of jargon speaks of, at best, an inherent snobbery and, at worst, a very 'macho' approach to beer as the myth that women 'don't like bitter things' persists, perpetuated by both ignoramuses who know nothing about biology and cynical marketing people who want to divide us neatly, so they can earn more money.

Scientifically what frustrates me about this is that it's often largely irrelevant to what you perceive. Some beers can play tricks on you. For example, in beers where the fermentation has been halted before the yeast can eat all the sugar – whether that's because the alcohol level has got too high for the yeast to survive or a deliberate choice by the brewer to keep the beer's body sweeter and therefore more viscous – it can often mean that

a lot of bittering hops might be used in the brew but not be noticed on the palate.

Also, there's the issue of adjuncts, such as brews with vanilla in them. These will always taste sweeter because the vanilla masks bitterness and acidity and creates a perception of creaminess, or perhaps it's because the beer contains lactose, which is unfermentable and therefore also adds a milky, creamy sweetness to the flavour.

Anyway, I've digressed slightly from sweetness in beer. There are multiple perceptually sweet flavours in beer – which can encompass everything from barley sugar and dark chocolate to brioche and strawberry – and come from multiple sources. Not everything is directly sweet; for example, tropical fruit flavours can come from either fermentation or hops, but raisins, caramels, milk chocolate and other flavours are directly sweet and come from the malt but also from the level of alcohol that is produced in the beer, which manifests as a sweetness on our tongues because it tells us it's a source of easily bio-available calories.

The myth that beer was a replacement for potable water sources in conurbations around the world doesn't seem to be one that wants to go away. Water has always been widely drunk, it's just it wasn't considered important to record because it was free, not subject to taxation and unnecessary to record in things like household accounts, which is where we get a lot of our information about how much beer and wine was consumed. I'm not saying we haven't, historically, been a bunch of happy imbibers, I'm just saying that the idea that 'beer replaced water because it wasn't safe' is basically hooey.

Acid in the House

One of the major benefits of beer is that it is naturally acidic – below 4.4pH – and, along with a cocktail of other factors (including hops, ethanol, low oxygen, high carbon dioxide and a lack of nutrients), this makes it incredibly hard, if not nigh on impossible, for pathogenic substances to survive; it is certainly well below the antimicrobial threshold. This means that while a beer can unintentionally go sour, or taste awful, it is really, really unlikely to cause you any serious harm – handy if you are, say, about to sail around the world nicking other people's countries and won't have a lot of access to safe drinking water on the journey.

However, you will increasingly hear the phrase 'sour beers' these days, and here we are generally talking about styles that are deliberately made that way. We perceive sour when hydrogen ions are split off by an acid dissolved in a watery solution and the main souring agents in beer are bacteria, which turn up in different forms in different beers.

Lactobacillus (Lacto) and *Pediococcus* (Pedio) are the two most important bacteria in sour beer production and, pernicious little buggers that they are, will find their way into beer via a number of different routes.

Lacto is the most straightforward one to address, and probably the predominant acidic note in modern beers at the moment, as it's what is used in beer styles like gose and Berliner weisse. It is also present in mixed fermentation beers and traditional styles like lambic.

There it takes a lot longer to make its presence felt, as it has to wait its turn after the standard fermentation with Saccharomyces yeast has achieved its level of attenuation (basically eaten all the sugars it can) leaving behind complex carbohydrates for everything else to munch on.

Pedio is also a lactic acid producing beast but, the problem is, it can also produce enough diacetyl to keep a cinema popcorn company in business for a week and can also produce a quite disgusting gloop called exopolysaccharides which, in extreme cases, can produce ropey strands in the beer, which are exceptionally unpleasant if you drink them accidentally – trust me on this.

A natural by-product of fermentation, diacetyl in beer can bring viscous mouthfeel at very low levels, a buttery caramel note in acceptable levels and smell like cinema popcorn at unacceptably high levels. It is also added to some foods to produce a buttery caramel flavour.

However, in mixed fermentation beers, you will find that it's Brettanomyces that comes to the rescue, as it will happily slurp up all the nasty diacetyl and exopolysaccharides, and many brewers stand by the fact that this ropey beer early on will lead to a more complex flavour later on. Named after the Greek word for 'British fungus', Brettanomyces (or Brett as it's more commonly known) was first identified by brewing scientists investigating British porters. Naturally present on the skins of fruit, it's a voracious beast that will not only gobble up the icky stuff mentioned but will eat complex sugars left behind during the normal fermentation process, leaving the beer very 'dry'.

The smallest sour contributor in the beer world is Acetobacter – the stuff that makes vinegar. This isn't the only way for acetic acid to turn up in beer, though. Brettanomyces also produces it in the presence of oxygen.

As a small aside, it's also worth noting that a lot of brewers are moving beyond just using a measurement of pH for sourness to acidic titration, which is something altogether different, as it is a far more accurate measurement of 'perceivable' acidity on your palate as opposed to the straight up 'physical' acidity that a pH measurement gives you.

How to Pair to Perfection

If there was only one piece of advice
I could give you about pairing beer and
food it's this: K.I.S.S.

Now, if that's made you land a
smacker on a loved one then great
but that's not what I meant (don't
consider it a pass to randomly snog
a stranger either!).

HOW TO PAIR TO PERFECTION

It's an old Army acronym that stands for Keep It Simple, Stupid. Now, please don't think I'm calling you dim – most assuredly I am not. What I'm exhorting you to do is keep things simple until you've got the training wheels off and, even then, experiment before you get too clever when presenting a new pairing to the person you kiss or others. And a big thanks goes to my darling friend Mike Hill, who shouted this at me when I was trying to disappear up my own fundament during an event planning session over a decade ago; it's stayed with me ever since.

Firstly, don't think you need to fork out some inflated sum on a fancy bottle from the nearest speciality beer shop to do justice to a beer and food pairing just because you think that by applying money to the problem, it will be solved (although this would almost certainly be my general approach to life if I had more money and fewer problems). Classics are classics for a reason; I strongly believe that there is absolutely nothing wrong with a top-notch lager with a kebab (in fact, it's what I've paired with my Lamb,

Haggis & Seaweed Kebab (page 107), there's little in this world to beat a sharp fruit beer with a rich chocolate dessert (page 184) and why would you even try to have anything but a pint of best bitter with a Ploughman's? (No, I'm not giving you a recipe for a board with bread, cheese, meats and a pickled onion on it; I'm pretty sure you can figure that out yourself, although the Beer Chutney (page 140) is a good accompaniment.)

However, that doesn't mean don't experiment. I've given both safe and unusual options for some of the pairings, the latter mostly stumbled across while aiming for something else. And because I have more experience than one woman's liver probably should have endured, please learn from my mistakes and get your bearings firmly on what it is you enjoy first and go from there. So, all that preamble aside, how do you actually start applying this strategy? Well, the simple answer is – come on, you know this by now – get to know your beer first (see Beer Styles, pages 22–23). But there is more …

Store-cupboard & Fridge Staples

Firstly, let me say, I know lists like these always look daunting and you're probably thinking that I've got some big swishy kitchen that has all the gadgets, a gigantic fridge, a utility room with a chest freezer and some sort of terribly British larder – I don't.

I live in a fifth floor, two-bedroom ex-local authority flat in London and, while I do have a lot of kitchen gadgets, I don't have the rest of the aforementioned and I've been threatened with divorce if I buy anything else – which, given the level of 'cupboard jenga' we have to play on a daily basis, seems reasonable... even if it is an utterly futile one!

I have a combined fridge/freezer, a two-level cupboard for condiments, a three-shelf corner cupboard that's two-thirds full of herbs and spices and baking stuff, and a small two-tier dry goods cupboard for rice, noodles, tinned tomatoes and other stuff like that.

They are also all totally disorganised and chaotic and I am not your role model in this regard!

So, to be clear, I am not advocating that you should go out and buy all these at once, unless you've had a huge clear-out and are looking to restock. However, some of these will turn up quite a lot in this book, particularly the 'used all the time' section, but build it up the way it suits you and your kitchen.

If you don't have a lot of money/time/space, then just cherry-pick the recipes you'd like to try and buy accordingly. The other thing I've found that works quite well is if there's a specialist ingredient that you don't want to lumber yourself with lots of, maybe ask a friend – they might be able to parcel something like pomegranate molasses out to you, kind of the modern culinary equivalent of borrowing a cup of sugar.

And, I may be presumptuous here, but I think most people have ketchup, various mustards and other condiments like chutney in their possession already, but please forgive me if you don't and add them to the list.

Used All the Time

Black peppercorns in a grinder

Chilli (hot pepper) flakes – if you grow a chilli plant, let some fruits dry on the plant, then whizz them up into flakes

Chilli pastes and oil – I always have harissa and a Chinese/Japanese/Thai chilli paste of some ilk and I love Taberu Rayu (a Japanese chilli oil)

Cooking oils – groundnut, rice bran or grapeseed oil (you can use cheaper sunflower or vegetable oil but they aren't neutral, which is how I'll refer to the first three listed throughout the book), basic olive oil and extra-virgin olive oil

Cumin – my most-used spice after chilli; I toast and grind seeds as needed, mostly because they last longer, but ground is fine

Curry pastes, various – I always have Thai green and red and usually rogan josh

Dark and light soy sauce

Dried mixed herbs

Hot sauce – my favourite workhorse is Cholula

Mushroom ketchup

Red miso paste

Salt – fine sea salt and crystal sea salt

Spice mixes, various – ras el hanout, garam masala and Chinese five-spice being my favourites

Vinegars – I always have malt, cider, white and red wine, sherry, balsamic and rice wine and invariably a Beer Vinegar (page 141)

Fresh Fruit, Vegetables & Herbs

Apples

Avocados

Carrots

Cauliflower

Celery

Cucumber

Garlic

Greens (kale, spring/collard greens, Savoy cabbage, broccoli, etc.)

Herb plants, various – the only reason my fingers are green is that they're potentially radioactive; I can't keep plants other than chillies alive, but even I manage to make herb plants last longer than little plastic packets of picked ones

Lemons

Limes

Onions – white, red and spring onions (scallions)

Potatoes – waxy or floury

Radishes

Satsumas, clementines or tangerines

Tomatoes (don't keep these in the fridge unless absolutely necessary)

Dry Goods

Baking powder

Bicarbonate of soda (baking soda)

Caster (superfine) sugar

Cornflour (cornstarch)

Dark chocolate (at least 70% cocoa solids)

Eggs, free-range if you can afford them

Granulated sugar – I buy unbleached sugars

Noodles, various

00 pasta flour

Passata (sieved tomatoes)

Pasta, various

Plain (all-purpose) and wholemeal flour

Plain and wholemeal bread (strong) flour

Polenta

Pulses – tinned chickpeas (garbanzos), butter (lima) beans, black beans (tinned, cartons or dried)

Rice – brown, sticky, risotto, paella, wild, black or white

Tinned plum and cherry tomatoes

Tomato purée (paste)

Vanilla bean paste

Vegetable bouillon powder

Wakame, a type of seaweed

STORE-CUPBOARD & FRIDGE STAPLES

I just want to take a moment to say there's a lot of unnessary pompous food snobbery around some pre-prepared or frozen produce.

A note on frozen goods: firstly, in all the outrage around things like pre-chopped vegetables or things like 'courgetti' or cauliflower 'steaks', few take the time to think of the less able. If your hands, if you are lucky enough to have them, aren't in 'normal' functioning order, how would you like to risk serious injury wielding a very sharp object around a spherical one just to make your dinner? Also, if you are cooking for one, isn't it better to be able to portion control than to waste food? And, of course, to people who are incredibly busy these time-savers are a godsend. Yes, there are packaging concerns around these products but being able to eat well is also important.

Also, a lot of produce is scientifically proven to be nutritionally better frozen than it is 'fresh'. If you think buying peas in a pod from your local store's fruit and veg section is 'fresher' than frozen ones, you're buying style over sense. Pick them straight from the garden, sure, but you're not getting more 'foodie' points for anything else, you're just getting rubbish peas.

Fridge

A lot of this will obviously come down to your chosen lifestyle. If you've got a food intolerance or are vegetarian or vegan then, hopefully, you will already be au fait with the alternatives you need:

Bacon – and a pot of saved bacon grease – don't judge!

Cheese – good-quality Cheddar, Parmesan, etc.

Dried chorizo

Milk – as an ardent 'builder's' tea drinker, this is always in mine

Natural yoghurt – I normally have both cow and goat's

Salted and unsalted butter

Freezer

Condensed leftover gravies, various

Fresh Asian roots and flavours – ginger root or galangal, kaffir lime leaves, lemongrass stalks (these aren't always easy to source and go off or lose their aromatic qualities quite quickly, so I always keep them frozen)

Ice – I know this sounds silly, but it's so annoying when you open your freezer to grab some to cool something rapidly – or for a G&T for that matter – and your ice cube trays are empty

Peas

Pre-chopped onions, garlic, ginger and chilli

Spinach

Stocks, various

Small pot of double (heavy) cream

Sweetcorn

Good to have

Allspice

Cardamom pods – black and green

Cinnamon sticks

Duck or goose fat

Marmite/Vegemite

Nigella seeds

Nutmeg

Nuts and seeds, various – salted peanuts, pistachio kernels, pine kernels, sunflower or pumpkin seeds and sesame seeds

Pomegranate molasses

Roast garlic

Smoked paprika

Sichuan peppercorns

Sweet potatoes

Tahini

STORE-CUPBOARD & FRIDGE STAPLES

Most-used Bits of Kit

These are the backbone of my cooking outside of the obvious hob and oven. I've only included things on the must-have list that I use at least three time a week when I'm just pottering around the kitchen on a personal level; anything else is a bonus.

Must-Have Equipment

25 cm (10 in) frying pan (skillet) with lid

10 litres (340 fl oz/40 cups) saucepan with lid

All sizes of plastic tubs

Bottle opener

Bullet-style blender

Colander

Deep roasting tin (pan) as big as your oven can fit

Digital probe (I favour the ones with a wire from the reader to the probe rather than the pen sort) and oven thermometer – I can't recommend these enough

Digital weighing scales

Fine sieve

Fish slice

Food processor – I love my Cuisinart

Good bread knife – mine's rubbish and frequently tries to savage my hand, so I speak from experience

Good chef's knife – go into a shop and try the different lengths and sizes and find what works for you

Grater

Hand-held blender

Hand-held mandoline

Heavy baking pan and baking tray (sheet)

Large and small chopping boards

Large sheet of muslin (cheesecloth)

Loaf pan

Lots of tea (dish) and hand towels

Medium-sized non-stick frying pan (skillet)

Metal mixing bowls

Milk/gravy pan with pouring lip

Wok

Pestle and mortar

Potato ricer – far superior to a masher and you can use it to make spätzle and similar

Ramekins (custard cups) – at least six

Robust apron with a pocket

Robust casserole dish (Dutch oven) or tagine

Rubber-edged boards with a small 'moat' on them

Silicone spatula

Speed peeler

Spoon rests

Stand mixer – I have a Kitchen Aid due to its durability and extra gadgets

Steel and knife sharpener – these can sometimes need to be brand appropriate due to the angle of sharpening

Trivet

Vacpac machine – a cheap one from a well-known online vendor is fine

Wooden spoon

Whisk

Highly Useful

Apple corer

Ceramic baking beans

Deep muffin tin (pan)

Flexible boning/filleting knife

Microplane grater

Pie and roasting pans

Pressure cooker

Slow cooker

Stovetop heat diffuser

Silicone non-stick baking mat

Springform cake pan

Vacu vin or similar

Specialist Items

Cream siphon

Ice-cream maker

Oyster knife

Pasta maker

Meat grinder

Sausage maker

Sous vide (this 'may' have been one of those slightly inebriated online impulse purchases, but I've never looked back – mostly as it's also a slow cooker)

Various silicone moulds in different shapes (see Pork Pie, page 162)

SO SIMPLE

Going back to K.I.S.S. at the beginning of the book, these recipes aren't always a 15-minute meal, but they're easy to make and should be a simple joy to prepare. From dips to indulgent mid-week meals and family recipes, a lot of these are dishes I can't imagine my life without.

It is an institution that,
when we get together on my side of the
family, there are dips involved somehow
and I won't hear a word against the
glorious simplicity of them.

These work by themselves, in concert
with each other – as they have the
common theme of earthiness and
cumin – or as an addition to other dishes
throughout the book, so if you make a
bumper amount you can use them for up
to three days later in other meals. I'm a
big fan of this approach because it saves
time, a precious commodity indeed.

Also, I strongly recommend that when
you're making dried bean or pulse recipes
you do add the asafoetida (hing); it's a
good digestive aid when eating legumes
and pulses, if you know what I mean …

Black Bean Dip with US-style Pale Ale
Serves 6

Ingredients

basic olive oil

3 medium-sized white, brown or yellow onions (300 g/10½ oz), roughly chopped

4 garlic cloves, crushed

½ teaspoon ground cumin

1 tablespoon Mexican oregano (or regular if you can't get Mexican)

¼ teaspoon asafoetida (hing) (optional)

6–10 slices of jarred, pickled jalapeños, roughly chopped (depends how hot you like it)

2 × 400 g (14 oz) cartons or tins of black beans, drained but not rinsed

¼ teaspoon fine sea salt, plus more if required

45 g (1¾ oz) US-style pale ale (I used Sierra Nevada pale ale)

grated zest and juice of 2 unwaxed limes

small handful of coriander (cilantro) leaves, finely chopped, to garnish (optional)★

★ *fresh coriander (cilantro) has been shown to be a genetically divisive flavour, hence the optional aspect*

After only ever having had terrible meals of pastiche Tex-Mex food in London, it wasn't until my much-missed, late friend Glenn Payne introduced me to the delights of proper Mexican food that my eyes were opened. He even gave me a great cookbook on the subject as an unexpected present one day. I'd like to think he'd hoover this up with gusto.

Method

Put enough oil to cover the base of a medium-sized saucepan on a low heat, add the onions, and cook for 10 minutes until softened and translucent, stirring from time to time.

Once softened, add garlic and cook for a further 5 minutes, stirring occasionally.

Add the cumin, oregano, asafoetida, if using, and jalapeños and stir well. Add the beans. Cook gently for 5 minutes, stirring regularly.

Allow to cool for 10 minutes, add the salt and blend with the beer and lime zest (using either a stand or hand-held blender) until smooth.

Add half the lime juice and stir, then taste, and adjust the seasoning and acidity accordingly.

Spoon the dip into your chosen serving bowl and garnish with coriander leaves, if using.

Cook

Sierra Nevada Pale Ale – USA

Dark Star APA – UK

Odell 5 Barrel Pale Ale – USA

Sweetwater 420 – USA

Baird's Rising Sun Pale Ale – Japan

Pair

Fuller's Montana Red – UK

Philter Red – Australia

Jopen Jacobus RPA – Netherlands

Hackney Red – UK

Negra Modelo – Mexico

SO SIMPLE

Recipe photo on pages 45 + 51

Hummust Try This

Serves 6

Ingredients

2 × 400 g (14 oz) tins of cooked chickpeas (garbanzos), drained and rinsed

1 garlic bulb, roasted, and the flesh squeezed out★

45–60 ml (2 fl oz/¼ cup) classic German pilsner or Helles (I used Camden Hells)

1½ tablespoons ground cumin

juice of 2 lemons

1 teaspoon caster (superfine) sugar

2 tablespoons tahini

¼ teaspoon asafoetida (hing) (optional)

1–3 tablespoons extra-virgin olive oil

fine sea salt

For the swirly topping:

1 teaspoon harissa

a splash of olive oil

2 tablespoons finely chopped parsley

1 tablespoon toasted sesame seeds

★ just chop the top off a garlic bulb, place on a piece of kitchen foil big enough to wrap it in, drizzle with olive oil, wrap in the foil and pop in a preheated oven at 180°C (350°F/Gas 5) for 30 minutes or until the cloves will squidge out the top. It will keep for ages in the fridge

I love a bad pun, hence the name of this recipe – I blame my father, who is a master of the 'dad joke' as I appear to have inherited this uncontrollable urge to make terrible wisecracks.

Method

Reserving a few chickpeas for the topping, put the rest in a food processor with the garlic and 2 tablespoons of the beer. Blitz for 30 seconds or so.

Add the cumin, lemon juice, sugar, tahini and asafoetida, if using, and blitz a bit more.

With the blade running, start adding the olive oil very slowly so it emulsifies and becomes smooth, adding more beer if needed (it will depend on how damp your chickpeas are). You want a smooth, thick consistency.

Taste for seasoning and acidity, adding more lemon juice and salt if required.

Spoon into a serving bowl and add an extra drizzle of olive oil. Use a teaspoon handle or chopstick to drag a deep swirl pattern in the top of the hummus.

Mix together the harissa with a splash of olive oil and carefully pour into the swirl pattern. Place the reserved chickpeas on top, garnish with the parsley, then sprinkle with the sesame seeds.

Cook

Camden Hells – UK

Veltins – Germany

Bierstadt Helles – USA

Pilsner Urquell – Czech Republic

Moon Dog Beer Can – Australia

Pair

Beersel Lager – Belgium

Augustiner Lagerbier Hell – Germany

Maui Bikini Blonde Lager – USA

Birrificio Italiano Tipopils – Italy

Victoria Lager – Spain

Recipe photo on pages 45 + 51

Baba Ganoush with Vienna Lager
Serves 6

Ingredients

4 large aubergines (eggplants)

2 garlic cloves, finely grated

1 tablespoon tahini

2 teaspoons ground cumin

grated zest and juice of 2 unwaxed limes

20 g (¾ oz) Vienna lager (I used Brooklyn lager)

80 g (3 oz) thick, full-fat natural yoghurt (preferably goat's)

fine sea salt

good-quality extra-virgin olive oil

large handful of parsley leaves, roughly chopped

It was a source of much amusement on the internet when I asked the question: 'Everyone else asks their other half to 'open the windows because I'm about to set fire to some aubergines (eggplants) again, right?' – turns out I'm much more alone on this than I thought. If you're blessed with a barbecue or a pizza oven then use that by just setting the aubergines directly over the coals on an oiled rack. This has the added bonus that it's less likely to set off your smoke alarm.

Method

Blacken the aubergines over your gas rings, turning carefully with tongs. Alternatively, set your grill (broiler) on high and put a large baking tray (sheet) on a shelf, two rungs down from the heat. Prick the aubergines all over, then put them under the grill, turning them as the skin blisters and blackens until this has happened all over.

If the flesh inside isn't softening, move the shelf down a rung, close the door and put the oven on maximum temperature for 10 minutes.

Allow to cool for 5 minutes and then, wearing kitchen gloves, rub the majority of the blistered skin off the aubergines, just leaving some to give you that smoky flavour.

Put the flesh in the blender with the garlic and blitz until completely blended.

Add the tahini, cumin, lime zest and Vienna lager, and blitz again.

Add half the yoghurt, blitz, check for consistency and seasoning, then adjust with lime juice and salt as necessary.

Spoon into a serving bowl and finish with a good swirl of olive oil and a hearty sprinkle of parsley.

Cook

Brooklyn Lager – USA

Harviestoun Bitter & Twisted – UK

Thornbridge Kill Your Darlings – UK

Devils Backbone Vienna Lager – USA

Hansa Vienna Lager – Norway

Pair

Birra del Borgo ReAle – Italy

Mateo y Bernabe Santiago – Spain

Young's Special Bitter – UK

Firestone Walker DBA – USA

Baden Baden 1999 – Brazil

SO SIMPLE

Recipe photo on pages 45 + 51

Flexible Flatbreads
Makes 8–10 flatbreads

Ingredients

400 ml (13 fl oz/generous 1½ cups) warm (but not hot) dunkel hefeweizen

1 teaspoon caster (superfine) sugar, honey or maple syrup

14 g (½ oz/4 teaspoons) active dried yeast

2 teaspoons fine sea salt

350 g (12 oz/2¾ cups) strong white flour

150 g (5 oz/scant 1¼ cups) wholemeal flour

4 tablespoons groundnut, grapeseed or other neutral oil, plus extra to grease

I use active dried yeast. There is a difference between this and fast-action yeast – the latter can added directly into the flour, whereas active dried yeast needs reconstituting with warm water and sugar. I like the warmer, rich yeast flavour that comes from the active version but don't worry if you can't get hold of it.

Method

Put 200 ml (7 fl oz/scant 1 cup) of warmed beer (you should be able to stick your finger in and register that it's hot but not need to remove it immediately) into a jug and add your sugar. Stir until the sugar has dissolved, add the yeast, stir again and leave somewhere warm for about 10 minutes. When it's got a decent head on it, it's good to go.

Mix the salt and two flours together until well combined, then add the yeast mixture and oil and stir it into the flour. Add enough of the remaining warm beer to get a 'shaggy' (rough) dough.

Use a stand mixer with a dough hook or hand knead for 7–10 minutes, or until the dough is smooth and elastic. Wrap loosely in well in oiled cling film (plastic wrap) and place in a bowl somewhere warm to prove for 60–90 minutes, or leave overnight in the fridge. The dough should almost double in size.

You can cook the flatbreads one of a few ways: you can use a dry frying pan (skillet) – cook on both sides until golden – but a heavy baking sheet or stone in the oven on its hottest fan setting seems to work best for me. They should puff up like a pitta bread.

Trying to tell you how long to cook them for is very 'piece of string' stuff. You'll be able to smell and see when they are done. They should be nicely golden in colour.

Cook

I've not offered a pairing here as it's more about what you put on it than the bread itself that dictates the pairing.

Erdinger Dunkel – Germany

Eisenbahn Dunkel – Brazil

Weihenstephaner Hefeweissbier Dunkel – Germany

Franziskaner Hefe-Weisse Dunkel – Germany

Sly Fox Dunkel Weisse – USA

....

NOTE: The cling film (plastic wrap) helps to limit aerobic respiration in flatbreads, as this causes the yeast to create much more carbon dioxide and puff the dough up.

....

Quick Pickles

Once you've got the hang of the principles of quick pickling, you'll be off and running by yourself. Please be aware, however, that quick pickles don't keep; they're designed for fairly instant gratification. Do taste your pickling juice and adjust the balance of sweet/salty/acidic to your personal taste. Just remember to take into account how sweet/salty/acidic the fruit/veg is that you're using. Also, when brining anything, don't use metallic bowls as they can react with the brine to create an unpleasant metallic flavour.

Watermelon, Mint & Chilli Pickle
Serves 4

I love this with Fabulous Fried Chicken (page 104). Contrary to my advice on page 53, it's a little more robust than most quick pickles so you can make it about three hours ahead of eating.

Ingredients

15 g (½ oz/1 tablespoon) fine sea salt

15 g (½ oz/1 tablespoon) caster (superfine) sugar

1 teaspoon chilli (hot pepper) flakes (optional)

20 ml (¾ fl oz/generous 1 tablespoon) hot water

330 ml (11¼ fl oz/1⅓ cups) well-chilled cucumber or watermelon sour beer

50 ml (1¾ fl oz/scant ¼ cup) rice wine vinegar

½ small watermelon, chopped into roughly 5 cm (2 in) square-ish chunks

cold water (optional), to top up

10 mint leaves, chopped, to garnish

Method

Put the salt, sugar and chilli flakes, if using, in a large bowl and add the hot water. Stir vigorously to dissolve the salt and sugar.

Add the beer and rice wine vinegar, and then the watermelon pieces and, if needed, enough cold water to cover the melon. Refrigerate for no longer than 2 hours.

When ready to serve, drain the melon and sprinkle with mint.

Cook

Watermelon, Mint & Chilli Pickle (above)

If you can't find a cucumber or watermelon beer, use a Berliner Weisse or Gose like Ritterguts Original Berliner Weisse or Magic Rock Salty Kiss.

10 Barrel Cucumber Crush – USA

8 Wired Cucumber Hippy – New Zealand

New Belgium Juicy Watermelon – USA

Cucumber, Radish & Seaweed (page 55 top)

Original Ritterguts Gose – Germany

Westbrook Gose – USA

Magic Rock Salty Kiss – UK

Red Onion & Fruit Lambic (page 55 bottom)

Original Ritterguts Gose – Germany

Westbrook Gose – USA

Magic Rock Salty Kiss – UK

Recipe photo on page 52

Cucumber, Radish & Seaweed with Berliner Weisse

Serves 4

Ingredients

15 g (½ oz/1 tablespoon) fine sea salt

8 g (¼ oz/1½ teaspoons) caster (superfine) sugar

20 ml (¾ fl oz/generous 1 tablespoon) hot water

330 ml (11¼ fl oz/1⅓ cups) well-chilled Berliner weisse or gose

50 ml (1¾ fl oz/scant ¼ cup) white wine vinegar

½ cucumber, sliced finely on a mandoline (I prefer organic as they're generally less watery)

5 radishes, sliced finely on a mandoline (if they still have stalks or leaves, use these too)

1 teaspoon dried wakame seaweed

cold water (optional), to top up

This works really well in a burger in place of a traditional pickle and also makes a nice sharp addition to a rich bowl of noodles in place of kimchi or with salads in the summer – it's very versatile.

Method

Put the salt and sugar in a medium bowl and add the hot water. Stir vigorously to dissolve.

Add beer and vinegar, stir, then add the vegetables and wakame. Add enough cold water, if needed, to cover. Refrigerate for no longer than 1 hour before using.

Recipe photo on page 52

Red Onion & Fruit Lambic

Serves 4

Ingredients

15 g (½ oz/1 tablespoon) fine sea salt

4 g (¼ oz/scant 1 teaspoon) caster (superfine) sugar

20 ml (¾ fl oz/generous 1 tablespoon) hot water

100 ml (3½ fl oz/scant ½ cup) well-chilled sharp berry fruit lambic/sour beer

75 ml (2½ fl oz/5 tablespoons) red wine vinegar

1 large red onion, sliced finely on a mandoline

cold water (optional), to top up

I'm a big fan of raw onions, but they're a little anti-social! This still gives you that inherent 'oniony' character but is softened and rounded a little by the pickle. Good in coleslaws and salads, it's also great in things like a Beer-brined Steak Sandwich (page 62).

Method

Put the salt and sugar in a medium bowl. Add the hot water, stirring vigorously to dissolve.

Add the beer and red wine vinegar, then the onions. Add enough cold water to cover the onions, if needed, then refrigerate for at least 15 minutes but no longer than an hour before using. It's best to give them a little squeeze before you serve or they will express a lot of liquid.

NOTE: You don't have to waste the quick pickling brine. It can be used in salad dressings or to pep up a sauce – just don't leave it hanging around too long in the fridge!

Recipe photo on page 52

Proper
Scotch Eggs

I will never understand why the rest of the world hasn't
embraced the Scotch egg with the alacrity of us Brits … it is,
without doubt, one of the finest beer foods ever.

Proper Scotch Eggs
Serves 2

Ingredients

3 medium eggs, at room temperature

½ medium onion (50 g/2 oz/½ cup), very finely chopped

1 teaspoon freshly ground black pepper

½ teaspoon chilli (hot pepper) flakes, crushed

½ tablespoon very finely chopped sage leaves

½ tablespoon each of very finely chopped thyme, parsley and mint leaves

small knob of unsalted butter

1 litre (34 fl oz/4 cups) groundnut, grapeseed or other neutral oil, plus extra for greasing

50 g (2 oz) black pudding, at room temperature, finely chopped

100 g (3½ oz) sausage meat (breakfast sausage), at room temperature

100 ml (3½ fl oz/scant ½ cup) traditional bitter (you may not need all of it)

2 tablespoons milk

50 g (2 oz/heaped ⅓ cup) plain (all-purpose) flour

100 g (3½ oz/1 cup) panko breadcrumbs

Beer Mustard (page 136), to serve

Somewhere between a snack and a meal in itself, when you cut into a well-made Scotch egg and the yolk makes a lazy bid for escape, it's a source of instant salivation.

You can absolutely mess about with this recipe. Don't like black pudding? No problems, substitute it with extra sausage meat. Fancy going spicy? Well, then flip to page 134 and knock up some extra Rauch Chorizo or Smoked Porter Toulouse sausage meat mix and use that instead. Want to make it vegetarian? Use the Fluffiest Falafel mixture on page 65.

Cook ·········· Pair

Cook	Pair
Black Sheep Bitter – UK	West Berkshire Good Old Boy – UK
Kereru Brewing Silverstream – New Zealand	Alaskan Amber – USA
Goose Island Honkers – USA	Firestone Walker DBA – USA
Timothy Taylor's Landlord – UK	Deschutes Bachelor ESB – USA
Magic Hat Barroom Hero – USA	Tsai's Bitter – Taiwan

NOTE: Your digital thermometer is really important here. You can just drop a cube of bread in and if it instantly sizzles then it's about the right temperature but this doesn't allow you to monitor your temperatures and you can burn the outside before cooking the meat, which is dangerous.

Method

Put a saucepan of salted water on to boil.

Fill a large bowl with cold water. Put the ice cubes in it.

Place 2 of the eggs in the boiling water for 4½ minutes, remove with a slotted spoon and put straight into the iced water.

Gently fry the onion, pepper, chilli and herbs in the butter over a low heat for about 8 minutes until the onion is softened.

Place the onion and herb mixture in a bowl lined with paper towels, and put in the freezer to cool for 10 minutes.

Take the onion and herb mix out of the freezer and remove the paper towels. Rub your hands with a little oil and squidge the black pudding and sausage meat together (it's joyously mucky this bit!) with the onion mix, slowly add the beer a splash at a time, making sure you don't make it too sloppy a paste and that there are still small chunks of whole black pudding. Pop the bowl into the freezer for 20 minutes to infuse and become firmer.

Peel the chilled boiled eggs carefully (see tip).

Whisk together the remaining egg and the milk and pour into a medium-sized shallow dish. Put the flour and breadcrumbs on 2 separate plates.

Take a 30 cm (12 in) piece of cling film (plastic wrap), oil it lightly, then place half the meat mixture on it. Lightly flour one of the carefully peeled egg and place it in the centre of the meat then, using the cling film, very gently mould the mixture around the egg, twisting the cling film closed once you're done.

Repeat with the other egg. Place in the freezer for 10 minutes to firm up.

Heat the oil in a large pan or deep-fat fryer to 170°C (340°F).

Remove the eggs from the freezer, unwrap and roll in the flour, then the egg and milk mixture and then the breadcrumbs, using one hand for wet and one hand for dry. Repeat at least once on both eggs.

Using a slotted spoon, carefully lower the eggs gently into the hot oil and fry for about 8 minutes, turning occasionally, until golden brown and the internal temperature of the meat is 69°C (156°F). This is a couple of degrees below the safe temperature but the eggs will continue to cook after you remove it. Be careful not to probe too deep with the thermometer and pierce your egg!

Place the scotch eggs on paper towels to drain and allow to cool slightly. To serve, cut in half and serve with your sauce of choice – the Beer Mustard on page 136 works very well.

TIP: The simplest way to peel a boiled egg is to firmly rap the more pointed end of the egg on a hard surface. There's an air bubble in there that will help lift the shell and membrane away from the white and make it easier to peel.

Recipe photo on page 57

Warm Kale & Nduja Salad
Serves 2

Ingredients

8 sundried tomatoes in olive oil, sliced into fine strips

juice of ½ lemon

1 red onion, halved lengthways and peeled, root trimmed but left intact

150 g (5 oz) nduja (if you can't get this, replace with a soft chorizo picante or other spicy sausage), skinned

2 tablespoons sunflower seeds

125 g (4 oz) cooked spelt or mixed grains (I use pre-cooked pouches available in supermarkets)

2 tablespoons classic saison (reserving the rest to serve)

50 g (2 oz) goat's milk yoghurt

500 g (1 lb 2 oz) whole-leaf kale

Nduja is a spicy, spreadable salumi, which originates from Calabria in Italy and a little goes a long way. This makes a great light supper or lunch, but if you want to make it a bit more substantial then add some griddled sourdough drizzled with some more of the oil from the sundried tomatoes and a splash of good balsamic. You can make this vegetarian by using feta tossed in smoked paprika or vegan by using smoked tofu and vegan yoghurt.

Method

In a small bowl, mix 1 tablespoon of the oil from the sundried tomatoes with 2 teaspoons of lemon juice to make a light dressing. Set aside.

Put a dry frying pan (skillet) on a medium heat. Slice the onion halves into 2 cm (¾ in) thick wedges. When your pan is hot, add the onions and cook for a few minutes until they just start to blacken. Turn them over and cook the other side. Place in a bowl and cover with kitchen foil to keep warm.

Wipe out the frying pan with a damp piece of paper towel, and return to the heat.

Take walnut-sized lumps of nduja and fry for a few minutes until they get a light crust on them. Add them to the bowl of onions and re-cover with foil.

Wipe out the pan again with a damp paper towel. Add the sunflower seeds and toast lightly on both sides, shaking the pan to prevent them from burning. When they are light gold, pop them in a small bowl and set aside.

In the same pan, warm the spelt on a medium-low heat, along with 1 tablespoon of the beer.

Stir in the yoghurt, then add another tablespoon of beer and the kale and stir through the spelt. Cover and cook for 3 minutes, stirring occasionally.

When the kale is cooked to your liking, give the mixture a good stir and spoon onto a serving dish or platter.

Sprinkle over the nduja, onions and sundried tomatoes, dress with the oil and lemon, then toss lightly. Check the seasoning and adjust accordingly. To finish, sprinkle with the sunflower seeds and serve with the rest of the bottle of beer on the side.

TIP: Place your serving platter, dish or bowls in a low oven during the cooking process so that the salad is lovely and warm when ready to serve.

Cook

Saison Dupont – Belgium

Amsterdam Brewing Bord du Lac – Canada

Karl Strauss Farmhouse – USA

Bridge Road Brewers Chevalier Saison – Ausralia

Tai Wai Beer No. 3 Saison – Hong Kong

Pair

Saison Silly – Belgium

Boulevard Tank 7 – USA

Brouwerij Martinus Saison – Netherlands

Brasserie Castelain Grand Cru – France

Fantôme Saison – Belgium

Beer-brined Steak Sandwich

Serves 2, easily scaled up or down

Ingredients

50g (2 oz) hand-hot water

25 g (1 oz) fine sea salt

4 fresh bay leaves, torn

6 garlic cloves, smashed

6 sprigs of thyme, lightly pounded

1 tablespoon hot sauce

500 g (1 lb 2 oz) coffee stout, chilled

450 g (1 lb) sirloin steak, preferably with a few centimetres (an inch) of fat on it

groundnut, grapeseed or other neutral oil, to coat

freshly ground black pepper

For the sandwich:

1 large or 2 small ciabattas (or other bread of choice)

handful of shredded iceberg lettuce, to serve

2 tablespoons of the Red Onion & Fruit Lambic (page 55) or finely sliced red onions (optional), to serve

ketchup or other condiments of choice like mayo or Beer Mustard (page 136)

Cook ········ Pair

Magic Rock Common Grounds – UK

Innocence Brewing Midnight Roast – Hong Kong

Mikkeller Beer Geek Breakfast – Denmark

Meantime Coffee Porter – UK

Left Hand Brewing Hard Wired Nitro – USA

Brooklyn Vienna Lager – USA

Brouwerij de Dolle Oerbier – Belgium

New Belgium Fat Tire – USA

Brouwerij Texels Skumkoppe – Netherlands

North End Brewing Amber – New Zealand

When you don't have a barbecue to hand, you can really miss that smoky char that you get on a steak at times, and recreating that flavour without setting off your smoke alarm can be a tough ask, so I came up with this as a way round it.

That's not to say this won't be excellent on a barbecue too, it will, you just might want to make sure your accompaniments are on the sharp and creamier side of things to offset the slightly bitter, smokier char you will get.

If you have any steak left over, then wrap it tightly in some cling film (plastic wrap) and use it within 24 hours in a something like a Thai noodle salad, a stir-fry or noodle soup.

One final note: it's always better to get one large piece of steak and slice it than to get smaller ones, you have more time to get a good Maillard reaction on the outside, which is at least 50 per cent of the joy of steaks. You can also serve the steak whole, as shown in the photo.

Method

In a large non-metallic bowl, mix the hand-hot water and sea salt until the salt dissolves, then add the bay leaves, garlic, thyme and hot sauce and stir for 1 minute.

Put the beer into the same bowl, stir briefly and submerge your steak in it, then add a little cold water to cover the steak if it needs it. Leave for at least an hour and up to 4 hours in the fridge.

Half an hour before you're ready to cook your steak, remove it from the brine and pat dry with some paper towels, leave on a plate to come up to room temperature and discard the brine.

Heat a large frying pan (skillet) over a high heat, until it starts to smoke slightly. Rub the steak on both sides with oil and place in the pan. Leave it alone, do not move it.

When the steak is one-third cooked through, turn it over, season generously with ground pepper. If you prefer it medium rare, when you can still see a thin line of pink meat (about 3 mm/⅛ in in the middle) take the steak out of the pan and place it on a warmed plate. Allow the steak to rest as you prepare the bread and other fillings.

Slice your ciabatta in half lengthways and arrange the lettuce on the bottom half. Pickle your onions (if making) and gather your various condiments.

Arrange your steak on top of the lettuce and season more if you like. Top with your condiment of choice and pickled onions, cover with the top half of bread, slice in half, as pictured, and devour.

··········

NOTE: When you're making sandwiches with any meat that has a 'grain' you should lay the slices so you bite across the grain, ensuring you don't end up with stringy bits that fall down your front!

··········

Fluffiest Falafel
Serves 4

Ingredients

300 g (10½ oz/1⅓ cups) dried chickpeas (garbanzos), rinsed

330 ml (11¼ fl oz/1⅓ cups) Belgian wheat beer

30 g (1 oz) each of fresh mint, parsley and coriander (cilantro) leaves, roughly chopped

5 good-sized spring onions (scallions), white and pale green parts only, roughly chopped (reserve the dark green parts to garnish)

4 large garlic cloves, pounded to a paste with a bit of salt

1½ teaspoons ground cumin

1 teaspoon fine sea salt, plus extra for seasoning

½ teaspoon harissa

enough groundnut, grapeseed or other neutral oil to cover 2 cm (¾ in) of the base of a large frying pan (skillet)

To serve:

lemon wedges (optional)

good-quality extra-virgin olive oil (optional)

toasted sesame seeds

There's no doubt that falafel has a bad name. Poorly done, it has a roof-of-the-mouth stickability that is second only to peanut butter but, done well, it's a crispy, fluffy ball of joy. I experimented with five types of beer versus water and the Belgian came out on top with everyone, offering bright citrus notes from its coriander seed and orange peel.

This recipe is a combination of J. Kenji López-Alt's recipe and that of a chef from my local Lebanese restaurant, plus my own beer twist. You can put these in a Flexible Flatbread (page 50) with some salad and any of the dips on pages 47–49 or just add a blob of natural yoghurt, a squeeze of lemon juice, a sprinkle of toasted sesame seeds and a drizzle of extra-virgin olive oil, as part of a meze or just as a starter. You can even pop them into a tagine right at the end if you like. If you check that your beer is vegan-friendly, then so is this recipe.

Method

At least 12 hours before you want to cook your falafel, put the rinsed chickpeas in a bowl big enough to allow them to swell to three times their original size. Pour over the wheat beer and top up with enough cold water to cover by at least 5 cm (2 in). Refrigerate.

Drain the chickpeas and shake off as much liquid as possible, blot with paper towels and leave to air dry, spread on a baking tray (sheet) for around 10 minutes.

Put the dried chickpeas in a food processor and add all the other ingredients apart from the oil. Pulse until the mixture resembles fine breadcrumbs, and the mix just about holds together with a gentle squeeze. Refrigerate for 20 minutes.

Form the falafel mixture into golf ball sized balls, and place on a lightly oiled plate.

Warm the oil in a large, deep frying pan (skillet) over medium-high heat. When ready to cook, gently lower the first falafel into the hot oil with a fork. Check it's lightly fizzing, not spattering, and that the oil reaches about a third of the way up (this should rise to halfway when more falafel are added to the pan).

Continue to add as many falafel as will fit in pan a few centimetres (inches) apart, turn the heat to high for 15 seconds and lower back to medium-high again. Cook for about. 4 minutes on each side, until golden brown. Repeat, if necessary, keeping the first batch covered in a warm oven.

When cooked, drain the falafels on paper towel, sprinkle with some lemon juice, if you like, a splash of good-quality olive oil, if using, and some salt. Garnish with green spring onion tops and sesame seeds and enjoy warm (not hot).

....

NOTE: You can freeze the cooked falafel for up to 3 months, reheat them for 15–20 minutes in a preheated oven at 175°C (350°F/Gas 4).

....

Tropical Prawns with Black Thai Rice

Serves 2 as a main or 4 as a starter

Ingredients

1 tablespoon Thai red curry paste

300 g (10½ oz) peeled, raw tiger prawns (shrimp)

4 spring onions (scallions), white parts finely chopped and green parts reserved for salad

1 tablespoon fish sauce

1 teaspoon cornflour (cornstarch), mixed to a paste with a splash of the below beer

100 ml (3½ fl oz/scant ½ cup) tropical fruit beer (not too bitter)

groundnut, grapeseed or other neutral oil

For the salad and rice:

1 ripe papaya (paw paw), cut into 2 cm (¾ in) cubes

½ cucumber, cut into 2 cm (¾ in) cubes

1 ripe avocado, cut into 2 cm (¾ in) cubes

a large bunch of mixed basil, mint and coriander (cilantro) leaves, finely chopped

1 teaspoon fish sauce

1 teaspoon sour fruit beer

150 g (5 oz/heaped ¾ cup) black rice, cooked to the packet instructions, then cooled and refrigerated immediately

green parts of the spring onions (scallions), to garnish

For the dressing:

20 ml (¾ fl oz/generous 1 tablespoon) tropical fruit beer (not too bitter)

40 ml (1½ fl oz/3 tablespoons) groundnut, grapeseed or other neutral oil

grated zest and juice of 1 unwaxed lime

1 teaspoon fish sauce

Obviously, the more local and in season you can get fruits the better. I am a huge advocate of that, but – confession time – I'm also a massive hypocrite because sometimes, in winter particularly, I need some sunshine in my life and this provides the illusion of it in spades. Make sure you look for ethically-sourced prawns (shrimps). Frozen are also fine but just allow time to defrost in the fridge.

If you can't find a tropical fruit beer then try a watermelon or cucumber version. And if you can't find black rice, substitute it out for whatever grain you have to hand. Alternatively, turn this into a starter or light lunch by leaving out the rice altogether. This is just a canvas – use it to make your own sunny painting.

Method

Mix the dressing ingredients together and refrigerate.

Mix the Thai red curry paste in a bowl with a little oil to soften it, toss prawns in it until coated.

Put a wok on high heat and, as soon it starts to smoke, add the prawns. Toss the prawns a few times and then take the pan off the heat for a moment. Add the white parts of the spring onions, fish sauce and cornflour, toss a few times, then add the beer.

Stir or toss again, then return the wok to a low heat for a few minutes. Turn off the heat and leave to rest in the pan while you make the salad and rice.

To make the salad, toss the papaya, cucumber and avocado and herbs in the fish sauce and beer, then arrange on top of the cold black rice in a bowl.

Add as much of the dressing as you want to the still-warm seafood. Toss a few times, then pour the prawns and the dressing over the salad and rice, and garnish with the green spring onion tops.

....

TIP: You could make this veggie/vegan by using same amount of firm tofu, and replacing the fish sauce with light soy sauce.

....

Cook

Ballast Point Even Keel Mango – USA

Matso's Mango Beer – Australia

YellowBelly Castaway – Ireland

Phillips Brewing Solaris – Canada

Lohnbier Catharina Sour – Brazil

Pair

Beavertown Neck Oil – UK

Founder's All Day IPA – USA

Young Henry's Newtowner – Australia

Hawkshead NZPA – UK

Epic Pale Ale – New Zealand

My Mum's Spag Bol
Serves 8–10

Ingredients

For the Bolognese:

1 kg (2 lb 4 oz) onions, finely chopped

4 large carrots, peeled and roughly chopped

2 courgettes (zucchini), peeled and roughly chopped

2 celery sticks, roughly chopped

1 large garlic bulb, cloves separated and peeled

olive oil, to cook

1.5 kg (3 lb 5 oz) minced (ground) beef, minimum 10% fat (if you want to use a meat replacement product here, then please do)

fine sea salt

1 litre (34 fl oz/4 cups) passata (sieved tomatoes)

800 g (1 lb 12 oz) tinned tomatoes

200 g (7 oz) tomato purée (paste)

500 ml (17 fl oz/2 cups) German hefeweizen

pinch of sugar

1 heaped tablespoon dried mixed herbs

2 teaspoons dried oregano

½ teaspoon whole black peppercorns, pounded in a pestle and mortar

1 tablespoon chilli (hot pepper) flakes

To serve:

2 x 500 g (1 lb 2 oz) packet of wholewheat spaghetti

a few torn basil leaves

Parmesan or Pecorino (or vegetarian alternative), shaved or grated

extra-virgin olive oil, to drizzle

sea salt and freshly ground black pepper

Before anyone says anything, this is not authentic and nor is it supposed to be; this is one of those comforting family recipes I learned from my Mum that I have changed and evolved over the years to being (roughly) what it is now.

Rather counter-intuitively, this has been the hardest recipe to write because I've never had to record the measurements before. I watched my Mum cook it, then I helped her cook it and now I cook it through the basic method of 'chuck in a load of that, a pinch of that and some of that too'.

However, the one thing that has elevated it, in my opinion (although obviously my Mum's is already perfect), is the use of a German hefeweizen because both the aroma of tomato vines and German wheat beers, due to the yeast strain, share a lot of common, or similar, aroma and flavour compounds and therefore intensify each other.

I hope that this becomes the kind of family staple that gets passed down through generations, morphing as it goes.

Cook ———— Pair

Cook	Pair
Schneider Weisse Tap 7 – Germany	Saison Dupont – Belgium
Ayinger Bräu-Weisse – Germany	Weihenstephan Kristall Weissbier – Germany
Widmer Hefeweizen – USA	Maisel's Weisse Kristall – Germany
Sierra Nevada Kellerweis – USA	Saint Arnold Weedwacker – USA
Bohemia 14 Weiss – Brazil	Seasons Basilicow – Brazil

Recipe method and photo overleaf

....

NOTE: Don't waste your olive oil by adding it to the pan to 'stop the pasta sticking' – it's nonsense, it just floats on the surface. Make sure the water is boiling vigorously and coming back to the boil after pasta is added, then turn it down to a frisky simmer, stirring well after a couple of minutes cooking. This dislodges some of the sticky starch that's formed on the surface.

....

Method

Put the onions, carrots, courgettes, celery and garlic in a food processor and blitz up very finely.

Take a large frying pan (skillet) and heat until it smokes. Add a tablespoon of olive oil, allow to heat for 30 seconds or so and then fry the minced beef in batches. Fry until the mince is a deep brown colour, seasoning very lightly with fine sea salt as you go. Remember to carefully wipe out the pan with a paper towel between each batch and allow the pan to come back to temperature, adding a tablespoon of oil each time. Remove the meat from the frying pan and place in the large cooking pot.

When all the meat is browned, add a little more oil in the pan and turn the heat down to medium-high. Add the blitzed vegetables and cook until it is just starting to brown (again, you may need to do this in batches). Put the cooked vegetables in the same cooking pot as the beef.

Place the pot over a medium heat and add the rest of your Bolognese ingredients, stirring well to incorporate them all. Bring to the boil for a minute and then lower to a simmer.

Half cover the pan with a lid and cook, stirring occasionally to make sure the Bolognese doesn't catch. Allow the sauce to simmer for at least 90 minutes. Check for seasoning and adjust accordingly but remember to slightly under-salt as the cheese and pasta will add some for you.

Cook the spaghetti in plenty of well-salted water until al dente, drain, then return immediately to the pan. Drizzle with olive oil, season lightly with salt and pepper and toss together.

To serve, toss the meat and spaghetti together, then spoon into warmed bowls. Finish with a few shavings of cheese, some fresh basil leaves and an extra grind of black pepper.

Versatile Beer-poached Chicken
Serves 4

Ingredients

1.5 kg (3 lb 5 oz) whole chicken

neutral oil and melted butter, for brushing (optional)

fine sea salt

For the poaching liquid:

2 × 500 ml (17 fl oz/2 cups) gruit or other beer with negligible bitterness like a Belgian wheat beer

3 large or 6 small bay leaves

2 carrots, peeled and roughly chopped

2 celery sticks, roughly chopped

handful of parsley leaves

1 garlic bulb, cut in half horizontally (don't worry about skins, just chuck them in)

½ lemon, halved

1 large red chilli (not too hot), pierced in several places

1 onion, quartered (don't bother to skin)

1 tablespoon dried wakame seaweed (optional)

1 tablespoon red miso paste

enough water to top up

There are so many ways to play about with this recipe, so I've used the most common way I make it and you can take it from there. It also flies in the face of most conventional wisdom about poaching chicken, because it starts cold and never gets above the softest of bare simmers. This takes more time but also means you aren't drying out the meat with high heat, giving a juicer result.

You can cook this a number of ways, a slow cooker on low being the obvious one, but you only want the chicken to internally hit 75°C (167°F) so, please do use a digital probe thermometer with a long wire (page 41), as it means you can accurately test the temperature by leaving it in the thickest bit of the thigh, and you don't have to keep poking holes in the chicken.

You can, also using an oven thermometer, set the oven to 90°C (195°F/Gas ¼–½) and then, after you've put the chicken in, turn down very slightly until your oven thermometer reads 80°C (176°F/Gas ¼) and leave for about 3 hours. Alternatively, you can use your hob (a heat-diffusing plate is handy here) on a low heat with the temperature probe in place.

Method

Place all the poaching ingredients into a large saucepan with a lid or your slow cooker and make sure the miso is well dissolved by stirring vigorously. Put the chicken, breast-side down, into the liquid and gently cook using your chosen method until the thermometer reaches 75°C (167°F) – roughly 50–70 minutes, depending on the size of the chicken. Leave to cool in the poaching liquor for about 30 minutes before handling.

If, like me, you think crispy brown chicken skin is everything, pat the skin all over with paper towels, brush lightly with a mixture of neutral oil and melted butter, sprinkle with fine sea salt and stick into a preheated oven at 200°C (400°F/Gas 6) for about 20 minutes, but watch it carefully so it doesn't burn.

....

NOTE: You'll notice there isn't any salt in the poaching part of the recipe. It's because you want to be able to use the cooking liquor as a stock, which will mean it needs reducing, and if you add salt at the start you can't subtract it. I know you may have heard that 'adding a potato will make things less salty' but that's not true. So, trust the old adage that it's easier to add than to subtract, and leave the salt out until the end.

....

Cook

I've not offered any pairings here because what you serve the chicken with will make all the difference – just keep in mind my earlier advice about pairing on pages 32–33.

Williams Bros Fraoch – UK

Jopen Koyt – Netherlands

Goose Island 312 – USA

Yoho Brewing Suiyoubi no Neko – Japan

Jing-A Mandarin Wheat – China

Blue Moon Original – USA

Estrella Inedit – Spain

Baladin Isaac – Italy

St Bernardus Wit – Belgium

Feral White – Australia

Celeriac Croquettes with Hefeweizen Sauce

Makes 8–10 croquettes to serve 4

Ingredients

For the croquettes:

1 garlic bulb

olive oil, to drizzle

600 g (1 lb 5 oz) celeriac (celery root) bulb, peeled and chopped

450 g (1 lb) floury potatoes, peeled and chopped

20 g (¾ oz) Gruyère, Comte (or a veggie or vegan equivalent), grated

1 teaspoon each of finely chopped rosemary, thyme and sage leaves

enough plain (all-purpose) flour to cover a plate

2 medium eggs, beaten

100 g (3½ oz/2 cups) panko breadcrumbs

1 litre (34 fl oz/4 cups) groundnut, grapeseed or other neutral oil, for frying

fine sea salt and freshly ground black pepper

For the sauce:

1 tablespoon good-quality extra-virgin olive oil

4 shallots, medium-finely diced

1 garlic clove, pounded to a paste with a little salt

1 teaspoon smoked paprika (or to taste)

100 g (3½ oz/2 cups) hefeweizen

2 x 400 g (14 oz) tins of cherry tomatoes

1 teaspoon grated orange zest

1 teaspoon sugar

1 tablespoon sherry vinegar, or more if required

I am a big fan of lazy dinners. This is can be made ahead until the frying stage or you can make double what you need and freeze the uncooked croquettes. I also like to serve this with a big side salad.

The sauce is actually really versatile, and something I keep in batches in the freezer to use as a quick sauce for pasta, a ready-made base for a bean or vegetable stew or even as a sauce for a quick cheat's pizza, using the Flexible Flatbread recipe (page 50) as a base.

If you'd like to make this recipe vegan, first source a vegan hefeweizen (this is cloudy German wheat beer, the name means 'with yeast') and then, for the croquettes, use 150 ml (5 fl oz/scant ⅔ cup) plant-based milk, omit the egg and replace the plain (all-purpose) flour with the same quantity of cornflour (cornstarch) – it's more sticky and will replace the egg's binding action. Then coat in the breadcrumbs as per the method instructions overleaf.

Cook

Ayinger Bräuweisse – Germany

Widmer Hefeweizen – USA

Schneider Weisse Tap 7 – Germany

Sierra Nevada Kellerweis – USA

COEDO Shiro – Japan

Pair

Bohemia 14 Weiss – Brazil

Weihenstephan Kristall Weissbier – Germany

Maisel's Weisse Kristall – Germany

Saint Arnold Weedwacker – USA

Moo Brew Hefeweizen – Australia

Recipe method and photo overleaf

Preheat the oven to 180°C (350°F/Gas 4). Chop the top off the garlic bulb, place on a piece of kitchen foil big enough to wrap it in, drizzle with oil, wrap it in the foil and roast for 30 minutes until soft.

Remove from the oven and set aside, keeping it wrapped in the foil to reserve the oil. Leave the oven on its lowest setting (90°C/195°F/Gas ¼–½)

Put the celeriac and potatoes in a large pan of vigorously boiling salted water and leave to boil for about 10 minutes until soft.

Line a baking tray (sheet) with paper towels.

Once the vegetables have boiled to almost falling apart, turn the heat off and allow them to cool slightly. Then carefully lift them out, place on the paper towel-lined tray and pop in the oven for 30 minutes to dry the vegetables out. It is best to use a fan setting if you can and leave the door open slightly if it's getting too hot.

While the vegetables are drying, make the sauce. Heat a frying pan (skillet) over a low heat, add the olive oil and cook the shallots for 5 minutes without colouring them. Add the garlic and cook gently for a further 5 minutes until the shallots are soft. Add the smoked paprika, stir well, then add the beer, tomatoes and orange zest and leave to cook on a very low heat for at least 30 minutes, stirring occasionally to stop it catching, adding a bit more beer or water if needed.

Season the sauce with the sugar and vinegar, adding more if necessary. Once cooked, remove from the heat and set aside.

Remove the dried vegetables from the oven and set aside.

Take a large mixing bowl and using the potato ricer, squeeze a layer of the dried potato and celeriac into the bottom of a bowl, add a little seasoning, a pinch of the grated cheese, a squeeze of roasted garlic, a sprinkle of herbs and continue layering in this way. (It's a bit fiddly, but it ensures a more even distribution of the ingredients.)

Add the garlicky oil from the roasted garlic bulb and mix together with a fork; don't overwork it, just make sure it's incorporated well. Refrigerate for at least an hour or overnight.

Place the flour, beaten eggs and breadcrumbs in separate shallow bowls. Use one hand for wet and one for dry. Form the mixture into 8 croquettes and dip them in flour, then egg, then breadcrumbs, making sure you cover every millimetre.

When you're ready to cook the croquettes, heat the oil in a deep-fat fryer or large, heavy-based saucepan, (the former is a lot safer and more reliable). Heat the oil to 180°C (350°F) or, until a cube of bread sizzles instantly when dropped into the oil.

Gently lower the croquettes into the oil a few at a time and fry in batches for about 5–8 minutes, turning gently, until golden. Drain on kitchen paper towels.

Serve warm with the sauce and enjoy!

Mid-week Mild Lamb Meatballs with Crunchy Salad

Makes 16 meatballs to serve 4

Ingredients

70 g (2½ oz/⅓ cup) quinoa grains, well rinsed, or 200 g (7 oz/heaped 1 cup) pre-cooked quinoa

neutral oil, for frying

For the meatballs:

½ red onion, chopped into chunks

2 garlic cloves

2 teaspoons ras el hanout

1 teaspoon ground cumin

1 teaspoon harissa

1 teaspoon fine sea salt

10 mint leaves

60 ml (2 fl oz/¼ cup) mild★ (reserve another 150 ml/5 fl oz/scant ⅔ cup for later)

500 g (1 lb 2 oz) minced (ground) lamb (around 20% fat)

★ *just to be clear here, mild refers to the type of beer not the flavour*

For the salad:

4 large carrots, peeled and shaved into ribbons

2 large courgettes (zucchini), shaved into ribbons

a few pomegranate seeds

handful of chopped mint leaves

For the salad dressing:

½ tablespoon tahini

1 tablespoon white wine vinegar

½ teaspoon fine sea salt

juice of ½ lemon

2 teaspoons pomegranate molasses

Firstly, please, please don't be daunted by the amount of instructions on this. It was a recipe tested by my Dad whose culinary skills, as I mentioned earlier, are only legendary because of his lack of them (sorry Dad, but you know it's true!).

And while we're on the subject of family, I find something oddly comforting about meatballs. Every time I look at them I remember my Mum cooking rissoles and rice for our dinner. Thing is, I didn't know they were called rissoles until my mid-30s. I was convinced they were called risseroles because I couldn't say rissoles properly when I was a kid, so risseroles they became and, god bless my family, they never corrected me.

Tales from the Cole household aside, you can easily halve the recipe, but I prefer to make more as the meatball mixture freezes well so you can just make half the amount of salad and the tzatziki will keep well in the fridge for a few days.

Cook ·········· Pair

Cook	Pair
Whistler Brewing Black Tusk – Canada	Padstow Brewing Sundowner – UK
Moorhouse's Black Cat – UK	Balter XPA – Australia
Black Tooth Saddle Bronc Brown – USA	Five Points XPA – UK
Speight's 5 Old Dark – Australia	Summit Brewing Extra Pale Ale – USA
Vale Brewery Black Swan – UK	Wild Beer Co. Bibble – UK

For the tzatziki:

½ cucumber, chopped into very fine cubes

1 tablespoon dried oregano

1 teaspoon fine sea salt

grated zest and juice of ½ unwaxed lemon

100 g (3½ oz/½ cup) goat's milk or Greek yoghurt

¼ teaspoon clear honey

75

SO SIMPLE

Recipe method and photo overleaf

Method

Cook the quinoa in boiling salted water according to the instructions on the packet, which will give you roughly 200 g (7 oz/1 heaped cup) when cooked. Allow to cool and set aside.

To make the meatball mixture, place all the ingredients except the minced lamb in a food processor. Add 50 g (2 oz) of the cooked quinoa and pulse until combined. If you don't have a food processor you can grate the onion and garlic and use a fork to 'mash' the quinoa.

Put half the pulsed mixture in a bowl, break up half of the lamb mince over it, then top with the remaining pulsed mixture and lamb. Combine the ingredients together gently; you don't want to turn the mince into mush. It should hold together when you squeeze a ball of it in your hand. Fry a teaspoonful of mixture and taste to check for seasoning. Adjust if necessary. Form your meatballs (you should get about 16) and leave on a lightly oiled plate, in the fridge while you make the salad and tzatziki.

To make the salad, put the carrot and courgette ribbons in a bowl. In a separate bowl, add the remaining cooked quinoa, pomegranate seeds and mint leaves and toss together. Set aside.

Make the salad dressing by putting all the ingredients in a clean jar, seal and shake vigorously. Mix in with the carrot and courgette ribbons, then put in the fridge.

Put all the tzatziki ingredients in a bowl, mix well and then place in the fridge until ready to serve.

To cook the meatballs, take the mixture out of the fridge.

Heat a large frying pan (skillet) with a little olive oil. Gently brown the meatballs on all sides, over a medium heat. Towards the end of cooking, deglaze the pan with a splash of water, then add 150 ml (5 fl oz/ scant 2/3 cup) of mild to the pan and gently roll the meatballs around in it. Cook for a few more minutes until it starts to reduce, then allow to rest for 10 minutes with the lid on. Give the meatballs one final roll in the pan.

Carefully spoon the pomegranate and quinoa mixture on the base of your serving plate then make a 'nest' of the ribboned salad in the middle.

Pop the meatballs on top of the salad, drizzle some of the pan juices over and then dress with the tzatziki. Serve with a cold glass of American-style pale ale, if desired.

Sardines with Beery Crab Meat
Serves 2

Ingredients

1 lemon

4 scaled, gutted, butterflied sardines*

10 g (½ oz/2 teaspoons) unsalted butter

2 tablespoons Belgian-style wheat beer

80 g (3 oz) white crab meat

1 large red chilli, finely chopped

2 large wild garlic leaves, finely chopped (reserve any flowers for garnish – optional)

60 g (2 oz) goat's milk yoghurt

large bunch of washed watercress, thick stems removed

fine sea salt and freshly ground black pepper

ask your fishmonger to remove as many of the tiny bones as possible, from the sardines – they are not nice to eat!

For the dressing:

6 tablespoons groundnut, grapeseed or other neutral oil

3 tablespoons cider vinegar

1 teaspoon creamed horseradish (or fresh and grated if you can get it)

pinch of sugar

One of the benefits of living on an island is an astonishing abundance of fish, and cold water oily fish is, in my opinion, the best in the world. You can use two mackerel instead of four sardines if you like and this is particularly lovely when cooked on the barbecue. This dish is also easily scaled up (as pictured on the next page), if you'd like to serve this as a larger meal.

Wild garlic is a seasonal ingredient but chives or garlic scapes make a good substitute.

Method

Preheat the grill (broiler) to its highest heat.

Make the dressing by mixing the oil, cider vinegar, horseradish and sugar in a clean jar. Seal and shake vigorously, then set aside.

Very finely slice half the lemon and lay on a roasting tray (pan). Reserve the other half of lemon for later.

Rub the sardines all over with butter and season the skin very lightly with salt. Put pepper on the flesh side. Carefully place the fish, cut side down, on top of the sliced lemons and set aside.

Heat a small saucepan over a medium heat and add the beer (it should cover the base of the pan). When the beer starts bubbling and is about to start evaporating, pop in the crab meat and gently swirl the pan. As the crab meat is gently heating, place the sardines under the grill until they are golden and crispy-skinned. Turn off the grill and leave them in the bottom of the oven to rest.

Take the crab meat off the heat and allow to cool a little.

Stir the chilli and garlic leaves gently into the beery crab meat, then add just enough of the yoghurt to bind it together.

Check for seasoning and adjust accordingly.

Place the watercress in a large bowl, drizzle with the dressing, then divide between the plates. Top with the sardines and a few roasted lemon slices. Dress with the crab mixture, garnish with the reserved flowers, if using, and finish with a squeeze of lemon juice and more seasoning.

SO SIMPLE

Cook

Dieu du Ciel! Blanche du Paradis – Canada

Blue Moon – USA

St Bernardus Wit – Belgium

Wäls Witte – Brazil

Fat Tire Belgian White – USA

Pair

Allagash White – USA

Hitachino Nest White Ale – Japan

Jeffrey Special Brand – Brazil

Fantôme Blanche – Belgium

White Rabbit Ale – Australia

Recipe photo overleaf

Beer-brined Pork Chops with Blue Cheese Polenta
Serves 4

Ingredients

For the chops:

30 g (1 oz/2 tablespoons) fine sea salt

100 g (3½ fl oz) hand-hot water

300 g (10½ oz) well-chilled sage, lemon or lemongrass beer

200 g (7 oz) ice cubes

2 preserved lemons, roughly chopped and any pips removed

2 garlic cloves, roughly smashed in their skins

generous 10 grinds of freshly ground black pepper

½ teaspoon chilli (hot pepper) flakes

4 pork chops at least 4 cm (1½ in) thick

groundnut oil, grapeseed or other neutral oil, to coat

juice of 1 lemon

10 g (½ oz/2 teaspoons) smoked butter (or ordinary if smoked isn't available)

4 sage leaves, finely chopped (roughly 1 heaped teaspoon)

For the polenta:

150 g (5 oz/1 cup) quick-cook polenta

600 g (1 lb 5 oz) water

½ teaspoon of fine sea salt

1 tablespoon basic olive oil

20 g (¾ oz) blue cheese of choice (I use Gorgonzola), finely diced

15 g (½ oz/1 tablespoon) unsalted butter, cubed

2 lemons, quartered, charred in the pork chop frying pan (skillet), for garnish

This is one of those recipes that you can prep incredibly easily for a mid-week supper treat. You can make the brine the night before you want to cook the pork, then place the pork in the brine and put in the fridge before you leave for work. Then the minute you walk through the door, take the chops out of the brine and wrap them in paper towel, on a plate, while you change and shake the day off. That way they'll be less cold when you come to cook them and it'll take you about 20 minutes to cook your delicious dinner.

The other bonus is that once the chops have been brined, you can freeze any you don't use, so you can pull them out to defrost and cook whenever you fancy. I serve this with curly kale or cavolo nero but you can use any greens you like, I find the bitterness a pleasant contrast to the rich polenta.

Cook .... Pair

Cook	Pair
Crooked Stave Colorado Sage – USA	Beavertown 8 Ball – UK
Hop Back Brewing Thaiphoon – UK	Schremser Roggenbier – Austria
Two Chefs Funky Falcon – Netherlands	Bear Republic Hop Rod Rye – USA
Partisan Brewing Lemongrass Saison – UK	Brighton Bier Co Downtown Charlie Brown – UK
Outer Banks Brewing Station Lemongrass Wheat – USA	Gage Roads Red Rye IPA – Australia

NOTE: If you have tongs that pull closed, then you can use them to hold the chops on their fat without having to hold them. Just grasp the chops with the fat facing down and pull the tongs closed and leave. Make sure you put the handle of the tongs over the handle of the saucepan though, or it all gets a bit hot! This is a good trick for rendering fat on steaks and lamb chops too.

Method

Put the salt and hand-hot water in a bowl, stir to dissolve the salt, then add the beer and enough ice cubes, to make 600 g (1 lb 5 oz) of brine. Add the preserved lemons, garlic, black pepper, chilli flakes and give the brine a good stir.

Put the pork chops in a large bowl or into a heavy-duty ziplock bag and pour over the brine. Leave to brine for at least 4 but no more than 8 hours in the fridge.

Drain the chops and retain 50 ml (1¾ fl oz/scant ¼ cup) of the brine. Heat the oven to its lowest setting and put a large plate in to warm.

Remove any tough rind from pork chops, keeping as much of the fat as possible, then score the fat halfway down in a diamond pattern. Preheat a frying pan (skillet) on a medium-high heat. Rub the surfaces of the chops with oil.

Without crowding the pan, cook the chops – two at a time if you need to – for about 4 minutes each side until well browned on both sides, then turn them onto the fat strip to render it. You may need to

turn the heat down for this bit to get proper golden fat.

Transfer the chops to the oven to rest. Turn the heat high under the frying pan (skillet) and deglaze the pork pan with a splash of water. Then add 50 ml (1¾ fl oz/scant ¼ cup) of the leftover brining liquor, the same amount of water and the lemon juice. Whisk in the smoked butter and bubble to thicken the sauce, stirring continuously.

When it's at the desired consistency, add the sage, pour into a jug and place in the warm oven. This is also a good time to put the serving plates in to warm.

Add the polenta and water to a pan with the salt and the olive oil and cook according to the package instructions. When the polenta is cooked, stir in the blue cheese and butter until it's all melted. Check and adjust the seasoning, if necessary.

Arrange the food on serving plates and pour over the gravy (minding the handle of the jug, it will be hot). Garnish with the lemon wedges and serve.

Moules à la Bière with Laverbread

Serves 4

Ingredients

200 g (7 oz) unsalted butter

1 head of celery, cut into 2 cm (¾ in) thick chunks, reserving the leaves for garnish

2 white onions, halved, then cut into 2 cm (¾ in) slices

5 large garlic cloves, very finely chopped

60 g (2 oz) tinned laverbread

100 ml (3½ fl oz/scant ½ cup) double (heavy) cream

grated zest and juice of 2 unwaxed lemons

1 bunch of dill fronds, very finely chopped, thicker stalk parts left whole

2 fresh or dry bay leaves

2 kg (4 lb 8 oz) mussels, scrubbed and de-bearded

1 litre (34 fl oz/4 cups) vegetable stock

335 ml (11¼ fl oz/1⅓ cups) bottle Belgian-style wheat beer

crusty bread, to serve

This is the very essence of simplicity – the active cooking time is about 20 minutes, and the only real elbow grease you'll have to put in is if the mussels need de-bearding. Lots of supermarkets now sell them virtually de-bearded but give them a quick rinse and a check.

Preparing mussels is easy. If one is open, give it a tap and if it closes, it's still alive and safe to cook; if it's not, throw it away. The beard is how the mussel catches its dinner – it's a filtration system so you just want to get rid of it because it's bitter and potentially gritty. You're looking for dangly greeny-brown bits poking out of the shell; give them a hard tug and they should come away.

If you're wondering what on earth laverbread is, it's bladderwrack seaweed, cooked down to a bright green blob and then packed into a tin. Seaweed is much under-used in Western cooking and is really very good for you. I won't use phrases like 'superfood' because that's dangerously close to 'wellness Instagrammer' bad science but it's something we could all benefit from eating more of, if for no other reason than it contains a dietary source of iodine. This is incredibly hard to get anywhere else and is vital for the health of your thyroid.

If you can't find it (I do have to order mine online) then you can replace it with 2 tablespoons of dried wakame seaweed, which you'll just need to rehydrate in some warm water and then blitz up. It won't be quite the same but it'll add that umami hit you're looking for in this dish.

Method

Melt the butter in a large saucepan over a low heat. Add the celery and onions and cook for about 5 minutes. Don't allow them to colour. Add the garlic and continue to cook gently for a further 5 minutes or so until the garlic starts to smell sweeter, still being careful not colour.

While the onions are cooking, mix together the laverbread, cream, lemon juice and zest and half of the chopped dill fronds (add the rest later if you like a stronger dill taste, it can be divisive). Tie the dill stalks with the bay leaves into a bouquet garni.

When the onions are soft, add the mussels and bouquet garni to the pan and cook for a minute, then turn up the heat to high and add the vegetable stock, followed by the beer. Cover and cook for a few minutes, shaking the pan occasionally, then cook for a further couple of minutes with the lid off until the mussels are just starting to open.

Add the cream mixture and allow to warm through for a moment. Pour into warmed serving bowls, sprinkle with the reserved celery leaves and extra dill, if desired, and serve with crusty bread.

Cook

Jing-A Mandarin Wheat – China

Du Bocq Blanche de Namur – Belgium

Nøgne Ø Wit – Norway

Baladin Isaac – Italy

St Bernardus Wit – Belgium

Pair

Jolly Pumpkin Calabaza Blanca – USA

Feral White – Australia

Magic Rock Salty Kiss – UK

Saison Dupont – Belgium

Gulpener Korenwolf – Netherlands

Sichuan Aubergine
Serves 2

Ingredients

½ teaspoon coarse sea salt

1 tablespoon Sichuan peppercorns (or more according to taste)

1 tablespoon dried wakame seaweed

450 g (1 lb) aubergines (eggplants)

75 ml (2½ fl oz/5 tablespoons) Flanders Oud Bruin/Red

1 teaspoon shop-bought Chinese chilli bean paste

1 teaspoon red miso paste

1 tablespoon dark soy sauce

2 tablespoons Chinese black rice vinegar

1 teaspoon clear honey

1 tablespoon cornflour (cornstarch)

1 tablespoon groundnut, grapeseed or another neutral oil

4 large garlic cloves, finely grated

1 thumb-sized piece of fresh ginger root, peeled and grated

5 good-sized spring onions (scallions), thinly sliced (or 60 g/2 oz), reserving the dark green parts for the garnish

cooked long-grain rice, to serve

I love Sichuan peppercorns and I love aubergines (eggplants) and this dish is a really simple mid-week meal that takes next to no effort at all – win! Don't worry about being too specific on the weight of the aubergines and you can always add more vegetables such as spinach, seaweed, water chestnuts, bamboo shoots, beansprouts or shredded Chinese leaf. Although it's incredibly mouth-numbing, it's not actually 'chilli hot' as a dish, and the rest of the Flanders bruin is perfect to go with it.

If you cook rice according to the absorption technique, then it will be perfectly cooked at the same time the aubergine is ready, so pop it on just before you start. It's easy to make this a vegetarian or vegan meal if you double-check the sauces and beers you buy to suit your chosen diet.

Method

Whizz the salt, Sichuan peppercorns and wakame to a powder in a small blender, (open well away from your face!).

Nip the green bit off the top of the aubergines, and cut into roughly 4 cm (1½ in) cubes.

In a small bowl, mix together the beer, chilli bean paste, miso, soy sauce, rice vinegar, honey and cornflour. Set aside.

Heat a wok until it smokes. Add the oil and the aubergine, and fry until brown and beginning to soften.

This will take a minimum of 5 minutes, so keep it moving so it doesn't burn.

Lower the heat to medium and add the garlic, ginger, white parts of the spring onion and Sichuan peppercorn mix, stir for about 30 seconds, keeping the mixture moving all the time.

Add the beer-chilli sauce mixture, stir well, and allow to simmer for 8–10 minutes, stirring occasionally, or until the aubergines are done to your liking.

To serve, spoon the cooked hot rice into serving bowls, top with the aubergines and garnish with the dark green parts of the spring onions.

Cook & Pair

You can cook or pair with any of the suggestions in the box – they're pretty flexible beers.

Duchesse de Bourgogne – Belgium

Rodenbach – Belgium

Liefmans Oud Bruin – Belgium

Petrus Oud Bruin – Belgium

New Belgium La Folie – USA

La Sirene Farmhouse Red – Australia

't Verzet Oaky Moaky – Belgium

Rodenbach Grand Cru – Belgium

Lost Abbey Red Poppy – USA

Thornbridge Love Among the Ruins – UK

Goat's Cheese, Prosciutto & Pea Purée Filo Cups
Serves 4

Ingredients

100 g (3½ oz) unsalted butter

4 spring onions (scallions), roughly chopped

2 garlic cloves, smashed

300 g (10½ oz) frozen peas

125 g (4 oz) bunch of watercress, roughly chopped, with any chunky stems chopped more finely

50 ml (1¾ fl oz/3 tablespoons) citrus or English-style summer or golden ale

270 g (9½ oz) pack of filo pastry sheets (have a damp tea (dish) towel ready to put these under the minute you open them)

100 ml (3½ fl oz/scant ½ cup) double (heavy) cream

grated zest and juice of 1 unwaxed lemon

200 g (7 oz) goat's cheese (I use 2 x 100 g/3½ oz rounds and cut them in half horizontally for 4 even portions)

50 g (2 oz) Parmesan, finely grated

4 slices of prosciutto crudo

fine sea salt and freshly ground black pepper

salad of your choice, to serve

This makes a lovely light dinner or simple spring time lunch recipe ... or is perfect for when you need reminding that one day spring will be sprung again and it can help lift your spirits. These little cups also work well cold as a packed lunch or a picnic item; handy if you want to swing by your local bottle shop, grab a few cold ones and then sit outside somewhere. I like to serve this with a simply dressed radish, cucumber, tomato and watercress salad but your salad preferences are your business. For a vegetarian version, leave out the prosciutto, make sure you get vegetarian goat's cheese and double check the vegetarian status of your chosen beer. You'll need a deep muffin or Yorkshire pudding pan for this.

Method

Preheat the oven to 200°C (400°F/Gas 6) and place a baking tray (sheet) in the oven.

In a pan, melt a third of the butter and sweat the spring onions gently for about 5 minutes until the onions start to go translucent. Add the garlic and cook gently for a further 5 minutes.

Add the peas and watercress and allow the watercress to start wilting, then add 50 ml (1¾ fl oz/scant ¼ cup) of the beer and cover with a cartouche (a circle) of baking parchment. Allow to cook gently for 3–4 minutes.

Meanwhile, gently melt the remaining butter in another pan and brush the inside of 4 holes in a muffin tin.

Take 4 sheets of filo pastry, cut each one in half, brush with the melted butter and make a star from the 2 layers. Gently push the pastry into the muffin tin moulds to make 4 cups. Place in the oven on the hot baking tray for 6 minutes until they are a light caramel colour.

While they are cooking, remove the cartouche from the pea mixture, add the cream and a squeeze of lemon juice and the zest and blend. Return to the heat if it's runny – it should be the consistency of rice pudding.

When the filo cups are very light caramel in colour, remove the pan from the oven and allow to cool a bit. Turn the oven temperature down to 160°C (325°F/Gas 3).

Fill the filo cups with pea purée, about two-thirds of the way up, top with a quarter of the goat's cheese, then with a quarter of the grated Parmesan and lemon zest. Repeat with the remaining 3 cups. Place the cups back in oven for 6–8 minutes.

Meanwhile, put a frying pan (skillet) over a high heat and dry-fry the prosciutto until it's turning brown and crispy. Transfer to paper towels, to cool and crisp up.

When the goat's cheese is gooey and the corners of the filo are turning a darker brown, remove the cups from the oven, break up the slices of prosciutto into random shards and stud them into the cheesey cups.

Place back in the oven for a minute and then take out to cool for a few minutes before easing them out of the pan with a flexible palette knife.

Serve the cups while they are still warm with a fresh green salad on the side.

Cook

Pair

Cook	Pair
Hop Back Summer Lightning – UK	Bath Ales Sulis – UK
Fuller's Oliver's Island – UK	Fourpure Pils – UK
Ska Brewing True Blonde Ale – USA	Firestone Walker Pivo – USA
Cricketers Arms Scorcher Summer Ale – Australia	Ayinger Lager Hell – Germany
Deschutes Twilight Summer Ale – USA	Budweiser Budvar – Czech Republic

Granddad Biscuits
Makes 24 biscuits

Ingredients

200 g (7 oz/1½ cups) currants

200 g (7 oz) best bitter (any fruity, nutty best bitter will do)

400 g (14 oz/3¼ cups) plain (all-purpose) flour, plus extra for dusting

1 teaspoon baking powder

250 g (9 oz) chilled unsalted butter, cut into 2 cm (¾ in) cubes

175 g (6 oz/scant 1 cup) caster (superfine) sugar

finely grated zest of ½ orange

¼ teaspoon vanilla bean paste

¼ teaspoon salt

2 egg yolks (freeze whites for use in a meringue recipe such as on page 181)

I loved my Granddad fiercely and we were all heartbroken when we lost him but I have such wonderful memories of him and this is one of them. They're called Granddad Biscuits because he was never without some in the larder and he used to rifle through to find me one that had the most obvious currants in it, saying 'that's a good one' as he handed it to me with a cup of insanely strong, sweet tea (I still drink insanely strong tea, just without the sugar).

Method

Preheat the oven to 160°C (325°F/Gas 3). Line a baking tray (sheet) with a silicone mat or baking parchment. Set aside.

Put the currants in a non-metallic bowl, add the beer and leave to soak for at least an hour.

Put the flour and baking powder in a mixing bowl, stir and then add the cubed cold butter and rub it into the flour until you get a fine breadcrumb effect.

Strain the currants and discard the beer as it will have wax from the surface of the fruits in it. Add the currants to the flour mixture, along with the sugar, orange zest, vanilla and salt and stir until evenly combined. Add the egg yolks and, using a palette or bread knife, cut the yolk into the mixture, trying not to overwork it too much.

When the yolk is fully absorbed, knead lightly into a dough ball and turn out onto a lightly floured surface, flour the rolling pin and roll out until the dough is about 5 mm (¼ in) thick.

Using a 6 cm (2½ in) fluted cutter, cut out the biscuits, gathering together and re-rolling the off-cuts to use all the dough. Place on the prepared baking tray in the middle of the oven and cook for about 15 minutes until just soft to the touch, keeping a close eye on them from 12 minutes onwards.

Transfer to a wire cooling rack, make a monstrously strong cup of tea and sit down to enjoy (I'm sorry, I can't recommend anything other than tea with these biscuits!).

Cook

St Austell Tribute – UK

Moor Raw – UK

Batemans XXXB – UK

Firestone Walker DBA – USA

Emerson's Bookbinder – New Zealand

Adnams Bitter – UK

Marble Manchester Bitter – UK

Birra Toccalmatto Stray Dog – Italy

Mordue Workie Ticket – UK

Alaskan ESB – USA

Quick Chocolate Pots with Kriek Cranberries

Serves 6 as a small treat or 4 indulgently

Ingredients

200 g (7 oz) dark chocolate with at least 70% cocoa solids, broken into pieces

100 g (3½ oz) spiced or barrel-aged stout

100 ml (3½ fl oz/scant ½ cup) double (heavy) cream

2 teaspoons basic olive oil

For the cranberries:

25 g (1 oz/¼ cup) dried cranberries

50 g (2 oz) kriek (see cranberries cook beers below)

2 teaspoons caster (superfine) sugar

tiny pinch of sea salt

Cook

Chocolate:

St Austell Tribute – UK

Moor Raw – UK

Batsman's XXXB – UK

Firestone Walker DBA – USA

Emerson's Bookbinder – New Zealand

Adnams Bitter – UK

Marble Manchester Bitter – UK

Birra Toccalmatto Stray Dog – Italy

Mordue Workie Ticket – UK

Alaskan ESB – USA

Cranberries:

Oud Beersel Kriek – Belgium

Odell Friek – USA

Boon Kriek – Belgium

New Glarus Wisconsin Belgian Red – USA

Russian River Supplication – USA

There are times when you just feel like you deserve a treat and these little pots are perfect. I had the idea when Tempest Brewing Company sent me some of its bourbon barrel-aged Mexicake – a kind of mole stout, and that's what I've used in this one, but there are plenty of other examples like it out there or you can substitute a barrel-aged stout – bourbon barrel ones work well.

Method

Prepare the cranberries first. Put all the ingredients in a small saucepan and warm over a low heat until the liquid just starts bubbling. Stir well, then allow to bubble for 4–6 minutes until the liquid is almost gone. Leave to cool.

To make the chocolate pots, melt the chocolate, using a microwave method, as on page 185, or a heatproof bowl set over a pan of simmering water.

While that is melting, put the beer in a small pan and heat until it just starts to bubble around the edges. Swirl the pan a few times but don't let the beer boil.

When the chocolate has melted, take it off the heat and add a small amount of the hot beer, beating with a rubber spatula until the mixture is smooth – don't panic if it looks granular, you just need to apply some elbow grease! Repeat until all the beer is used and you have a smooth, shiny paste.

Add the cream and oil and beat until you get a smooth mixture. Pour into espresso cups or ramekins (custard cups). Place in the fridge for 30 minutes to set.

Take out of the fridge, top with the soaked cranberries and serve.

SOME EFFORT

These recipes might be ones you cook with someone else, or pootling around the kitchen on a lazy weekend or day off. They aren't horrifically complicated but may call for either a little patience, or a little time, something we should all take a little more of for ourselves. Oh, and there are a few 'restorative' recipes in here too because 'bine flu' is real…

Spicy Bean Breakfast Tortilla
Serves 2

Ingredients

- 2 large tortillas wraps

- 150 g (5 oz) Berliner Weisse/Gose Cottage Cheese (see page 201)

- 150 g (5 oz) Black Bean Dip with US-style Pale Ale (see page 47)

- 2 tomatoes, chopped into eighths

- 100 g (3½ oz) chorizo picante or other spicy sausage, cut into bite-sized chunks

- 1 ripe avocado

- juice of 1 lime

- 5 good-sized mint leaves, finely shredded

- groundnut, grapeseed or other neutral oil, for frying

- 2 eggs

- coarse sea salt and freshly ground black pepper

- chopped coriander (cilantro), mint and parsley, to garnish

- hot sauce of choice (optional)

This is one of those 'restorative' recipes I mentioned earlier (page 91) for when 'bine flu' (hops grow on a bine, not a vine, so it's my nickname for a hangover) strikes.

Somehow – and I know I am entirely kidding myself here – this hangover-handling bundle of bliss feels a bit 'healthier' than a full English … it probably isn't but who cares when you feel like your brain is dribbling out of your ears?

The other bonus is, if you make pretty much everything the day before (or cheat with shop-bought cottage cheese and black bean dip), all you'll have to do is cook the tomatoes, eggs and chorizo when you arise from your pit – thank me when you feel better. This recipe can be easily scaled up, as illustrated, for a larger breakfast feast.

Method

Warm the tortillas on your serving plates in a low oven and take the cottage cheese out of the fridge; you don't want this to be too cold.

Put a saucepan on a low heat, add a little water to the bottom and add the black bean dip to warm up. Once warm, set aside until required.

Put a frying pan (skillet) on to a medium-high heat. When it's up to heat, add the chopped tomatoes (stand well back, this gets very spitty!), then add the chorizo and continue to cook.

Meanwhile, make the guacamole by halving the avocado, carefully removing the stone and scooping out the flesh onto a chopping board. Sprinkle with a little salt and pepper and mash to your preferred texture with a fork. Squeeze over the lime juice and continue to mash, checking for seasoning as you do, then stir in the mint and set aside.

When the tomato and chorizo mixture have cooked to your liking (you want the tomatoes to cook really well, until they are blackening for preference, but your choice), remove from the heat and pop in the oven to keep warm.

Put a second frying pan on the hob and allow it to get hot. Add a splash of oil to the pan and crack the eggs in to fry.

While the eggs are frying, take the tortillas out of the oven. Distribute the tomato and chorizo mixture, guacamole and black bean dip evenly between the wraps. Top with the fried eggs, sprinkle with the herbs and serve with some cottage cheese and hot sauce (if you're feeling brave enough!) on the side.

English Breakfast Congee
Serves 2, easily multiplied

Ingredients

For the cured duck egg yolks:

100 ml (3½ fl oz/scant ½ cup) Chinese black vinegar

50 ml (1¾ fl oz/scant ¼ cup) Worcestershire sauce

1 teaspoon gochujang or other chilli paste

100 ml (3½ fl oz/scant ½ cup) strong, dark ale

20 ml (¾ fl oz/generous 1 tablespoon) light soy sauce

2 duck egg yolks

For the porridge base:

400 ml (13 fl oz/generous 1½ cups) chicken stock

80 g (3 oz/⅔ cup) traditional porridge oats

1 teaspoon light soy sauce

For the toppings:

40 g (1½ oz) enoki mushrooms

50 ml (1¾ fl oz/scant ¼ cup) Chinese black vinegar

4 teaspoons light soy sauce

1 tomato, skinned, deseeded and chopped into 2 cm (¾ in) dice

100 ml (3½ fl oz/scant ½ cup) rice wine vinegar

25 g (1 oz) smoked bacon lardons (pieces)

2 spring onions (scallions), green bits only, roughly chopped, to garnish

30 g (1 oz) Cucumber, Radish & Seaweed with Berliner Weisse (page 55)

25 g (1 oz) spicy, thin salami, chopped into 2 cm (¾ in) chunks

a jar of Taberu Rayu (see store-cupboard ingredients on page 37), or other chilli oil of your choice

dark soy or fish sauce, to season

During a visit to Shanghai, I became a bit obsessed with congee for breakfast; I love it. I'm not someone who is big on eating breakfast when they first wake up but every morning I'd be up, in the shower and racing down to the hotel restaurant for my congee fix.

Congee is traditional, in varying forms, in about 12 different countries, so there really is no hard and fast rule about it and this is just my fun take on it.

You can very easily make this a vegetarian dish by replacing the chicken stock with water or vegetable stock and the meat with deep-fried tofu – personally I think the beer-cured egg yolk is one of the best things about this dish but if you want to make it vegan, that obviously has to go.

Method

To cure the duck eggs, first whisk all the ingredients (except the eggs) together in a soup bowl. Carefully lower the duck egg yolks into the liquid, cover with cling film (plastic wrap) and place in fridge for a minimum of 8 hours (reserve the whites to use in the meringues on page 181).

To make the porridge base, combine the stock, oats and soy sauce in a saucepan and cook over a low heat for 1–1½ hours, until it just bubbles, stirring occasionally and adding water if it gets too sticky. This should be a thinnish porridge.

Prepare the toppings. Cut the base off the mushroom and separate into individual 'shrooms. In a bowl, marinate the mushrooms in the black vinegar and half the light soy sauce for 15 minutes.

In a separate bowl, let the tomato infuse in the rice wine vinegar and the remaining light soy sauce in a separate bowl for 15 minutes. Fry the bacon without any additional fat in a hot frying pan (skillet) until crisp and golden.

Just before serving, warm some large, wide serving bowls in a low oven. Place all the condiments on the table in separate ramekins (custard cups) or small dishes.

Portion out the porridge, place the egg yolks in the middle, bring to the table and garnish the congee the way you like it.

Cook

Orkney Brewery Skullsplitter – UK

De Molen Weer & Wind – Netherlands

JW Lees Manchester Star – UK

Mateo y Bernabe Santiago – Spain

Stone Old Guardian – USA

Asparagus Two Ways with Fluffy Saison Hollandaise
Serves 2

Ingredients

1 teaspoon cider vinegar

2 sprigs of thyme

pared zest of 1 unwaxed lemon

5 voatsiperifery or ordinary black peppercorns

125 g (4 oz) unsalted butter

8 English asparagus spears

2 egg yolks

1 tablespoon ice-cold herbal saison or Belgian-style wheat beer

nasturtium flowers (optional), to garnish

fine sea salt

Cook ···· Pair

Any of the saisons will pair very well if you want a slightly less boozy option!

Saison Dupont – Belgium	Gouden Carolus – Belgium
Saison Silly – Belgium	Duvel – Belgium
Solo Beer Horiatiki – Greece	Ommegang Tripel Perfection – USA
Burning Sky Saison à la Provision – UK	Mikkeller Trippel A – Denmark
8 Wired Saison Sauvin – New Zealand	Adnams Tripel Knot – UK

I love spring in the UK – the trees are bent low with blossom, the cricket season starts and there's an air of expectation and optimism that's almost tangible. It's also such a great time for fresh produce.

Some of my most longed-for treats finally come to fruition in Britain in April and May and there is nothing, and I mean nothing, that compares to English green asparagus – sorry, but I'm not brooking any argument here. That Peruvian stuff you get in winter is flavourless, and don't even get me started on that weird white stuff in jars!

···········

NOTE: Very warm plates play a big role in this dish – make sure you prepare them in advance. You'll also need a griddle pan, steamer, a mixing bowl and a micro whisk. I'm warning you because, despite having quite a few steps, this recipe is actually quite quick to come together.

···········

Method

Warm the plates in a low oven.

Put a small pan on a high heat, add the vinegar, thyme, lemon zest and peppercorns and bring to the boil. Turn the heat off immediately and leave to infuse for 10 minutes.

Melt the butter in another pan over a low heat while you prepare the asparagus by trimming any tough ends. Skim any solids off the top of the butter, then leave it in the oven.

Strain the vinegar into a heatproof mixing bowl with the egg yolks and add a pinch of salt.

Start heating a griddle pan and a steamer. Put about 5 cm (2 in) of water in a pan that will house your egg bowl without it touching the bottom. Bring it to the boil, then lower to a simmer.

Add a splash of ice-cold beer to the egg bowl, place on top of the pan of simmering water and start whisking briskly.

Remove from the heat and start slowly adding the melted butter, whisking constantly until you have a rich, creamy hollandaise.

Place half the spears on the hot griddle pan and the other half in the steamer, then griddle or steam for 3–5 minutes (this will depend on the thickness of your asparagus – the stems should just yield to the tip of a sharp knife). Remove and place on a plate lined with some paper towel.

Take the hollandaise and add another splash of ice-cold beer and use a micro whisk to beat it into a lighter, more foamy sauce (a little coffee frother works well here too!).

Mix up the asparagus spears, pop them on your warmed plates, apply lashings of the hollandaise and decorate with the flowers, if using.

Eat with your fingers.

Chicken, Bacon, Cheese & Leek Pie
Serves 4–6

Ingredients

For the pie filling:

1 tablespoon groundnut, grapeseed or other neutral oil

500 g (1 lb 2 oz) skinless, boneless chicken thighs, chopped into bite-sized chunks

100 g (3½ oz) smoked bacon lardons (pieces)

1 white or yellow onion, finely chopped

2 garlic cloves, finely chopped

2 good-sized leeks, trimmed, washed and cut into 3 cm (1¼ in) discs

200 ml (7 fl oz/scant 1 cup) chicken gravy (shop-bought or from the Versatile Beer-poached Chicken, page 70)

1 tablespoon dried tarragon

175 ml (6 fl oz/¾ cup) golden or summer ale

1 teaspoon grated unwaxed lemon zest

100 g (3½ oz) mature Brie or Camembert (or local equivalents)

salt and freshly ground black pepper

For the shortcrust pastry:

500 g (1 lb 2 oz/4 cups) plain (all-purpose) flour, plus extra for dusting

pinch of salt

125 g (4 oz) unsalted butter, cold and cubed, plus extra for greasing

125 g (4 oz) lard, cold and cubed

1 teaspoon cider vinegar

a splash or two of well-chilled beer (use the same one as for the filling)

cold water

For the pastry lid:

320 g (11 oz) all-butter puff pastry

1 egg, beaten well with a splash of water

There aren't many things more satisfying than a bubbling pie and this was born out of my almost constant disappointment with how bland chicken pies can be – often claggy and lacking punch. I wanted to make this something special.

If you want an all shortcrust or all puff pie just increase the quantities accordingly and feel free to buy a ready-made shortcrust pie case or pre-made pastry rather than making it. This pie is great for using leftovers from a Sunday roast, Christmas or Thanksgiving.

You'll need a 20 cm (8 in) diameter pie dish or an oval one that's 25 × 17 cm (10 × 6½ in). I've also broken this recipe down into separate elements to make it easier to follow by stages, so if before shopping for ingredients, make sure you read all of it first.

Cook ········· Pair

Cook	Pair
Mountain Goat Summer Ale – Australia	Fourpure Session IPA – UK
Brooklyn Summer Ale – USA	Colonial Brewing Small Ale – Australia
Olvi Summer Ale – Finland	Tuatara Sauvinova – New Zealand
Doctor Brew Summer Ale – Poland	Amager Bryghaus Bryggens Blond – Denmark
Harviestoun Schiehallion – UK	De Halve Maan Brugse Zot – Belgium

Method

First make the filling. Put a large frying pan (skillet) over a medium-high heat, add the oil and fry the chicken pieces for about 8 minutes until just going golden. Then add the bacon and continue to fry, stirring occasionally, until the chicken is golden brown all over.

Turn the heat down low, add the onion and fry for 5 minutes. Add the garlic and cook for a further 3 minutes, then add the leeks and continue to cook for another minute until soft and translucent.

Add the chicken gravy and stir well to deglaze the pan, then turn heat right down.

Stir in the tarragon and the beer (reserving some for the pastry if making yourself), and simmer gently for about 15 minutes to reduce to a thickish sauce.

Add the lemon zest, remove from the heat and allow to cool for 10 minutes before putting in the fridge for half an hour.

To make the pastry, sift the flour and salt into a large mixing bowl. Rub the cubed butter and lard into the flour until it resembles breadcrumbs.

Add the vinegar and just enough cold beer to bring the mixture together into a rough dough. Knead gently but do not overwork. Wrap in cling film (plastic wrap) and chill in the fridge for 30 minutes.

Preheat the oven to 180°C (350°F/Gas 4).

To assemble the pie, roll out the shortcrust pastry on a floured surface, to twice the size of your pie dish, place in the dish, leaving any spare pastry hanging over the sides.

. . . .

TIP: Lightly dampen and scrunch up the baking parchment before trying to fit it in as this makes it easier.

. . . .

Cover the pastry with baking parchment, fill with baking beans and blind bake for 15 minutes, or until it's just beginning to colour. Remove the baking beans and parchment, then return the case to the oven for another 5 minutes. Remove and leave to cool for 10 minutes. Trim any excess pastry edges and turn the oven up to 220°C (430°F/Gas 7).

Put half the cooled filling in the pie, stud with torn off chunks of half the Brie, repeat with the remaining filling and Brie and season.

Roll out the puff pastry for the pie lid, to slightly larger than the top of the pie dish, brush the edges of the shortcrust with egg wash and place the puff pastry over the filling, crimping it to the shortcrust pastry base (I use a fork). Brush with more egg wash, poke a hole in the middle and place in the preheated oven (see photo overleaf).

Bake for about 25 minutes, egg washing again after 15 minutes if you want a deeper golden finish (any remaining egg wash will freeze in a small plastic tub). When it's ready, the top should be puffed and golden brown and the insides just bubbling through.

. . . .

TIP: For an alternative to bacon, try using the Gingery Ham from page 118 instead.

. . . .

SOME EFFORT

Recipe photo overleaf

Fabulous Fried Chicken

Serves 4

Ingredients

1.5 kg (3 lb 5 oz) chicken, cut into 8 pieces, or 8 skin-on chicken thighs

Watermelon, Mint & Chilli Pickle (page 54), to serve

For the brine:

700 ml (24 fl oz/scant 3 cups) hand-hot water

½ teaspoon medium hot sauce (I use Cholula)

3 g (⅛ oz) fine sea salt

1 tablespoon Cajun seasoning

7 g (¼ oz) smoked salt

1 fresh red chilli, roughly chopped

1 tablespoon dried oregano

1 teaspoon dried wakame seaweed

500 g (1 lb 2 oz) well-chilled strong, sweet, brown ale★

300 ml (10 fl oz/1¼ cups) cold buttermilk

1 medium egg, whisked

★ *keeping the beer well chilled makes sure you don't need to waste time waiting for the brine to cool*

For the coating:

500 g (1 lb 2 oz/4 cups) plain (all-purpose) flour

250 g (9 oz/2½ cups) cornflour (cornstarch)

1 tablespoon salt

1 teaspoon icing (confectioners') sugar

1 tablespoon Cajun seasoning

For frying:

1 litre (34 fl oz/4 cups) groundnut, grapeseed or other neutral oil

300 g (10½ oz) lard or vegetable shortening

For the seasoning:

2 tablespoons coarse sea salt

1 tablespoon Cajun seasoning

pinch of dried wakame seaweed (optional)

I've been to a lot of places in the world and I've eaten a lot of fried chicken because I'm always searching for the good stuff, and the first of the two places I've eaten the best is the Southerner in beautiful Sagautuk, Michigan. With a hangover the size of the great lake itself, my good friend Fred Bueltman took me to meet Matthew Millar, who not only makes amazing fried chicken but also cured me of the opinion that US-style 'biscuits' are all stodgy monstrosities.

The second best fried chicken I have ever eaten, and continue to enjoy, is in my hometown of London, at Chick 'n' Sours, which is also where I got the idea for the pickled watermelon. It's also the place that finally convinced my husband that fried chicken is, indeed, the food stuff of the gods.

Method

To make the brine, first put the water in a non-metallic bowl, add the remaining brine ingredients, except the beer, buttermilk and egg, and stir until the salt has dissolved.

Add the chilled beer and buttermilk, stir well, then add the whisked egg (it may look a bit grim at this point but don't panic, it's fine).

Put the chicken pieces in a large, heavyweight ziplock bag, add the brine, seal carefully (I generally double-bag mine) and leave in the refrigerator for a minimum of 4 hours, maximum 8.

Preheat the oven to about 80°C (176°F/Gas ½) or its lowest setting. Cover a baking tray (sheet) with a paper towel and put it in the oven.

Mix all the ingredients for the coating together in a bowl and set aside.

Get a large, deep flat frying pan (skillet), and add the oil, lard or shortening (I use 2 parts oil one part lard) – it should come about 4 cm (1½ in) up the side or about halfway up the thickest chicken pieces –

and put on a medium heat. Don't make it too hot or you'll burn the crust before you cook the chicken.

Remove the chicken from the refrigerator and coat it in the flour mix, 2 pieces at a time, pressing it firmly in the mix. Then re-dip it in the brine and repeat the dredging, making sure you get all the nooks and crannies covered. Lower the chicken into the hot oil; it should sizzle gently but satisfyingly, and not spit anywhere.

Repeat the double dredging with the remaining chicken pieces and add them to pan without crowding it. If necessary fry the chicken in several batches, allowing the cooked ones to rest in the oven on the lined tray as you go.

Blitz together the salt, Cajun seasoning and wakame, if using. Sprinkle the chicken with the seasoning and serve with the pickled watermelon and any other side you like.

....

NOTE: It's generally simpler to brine the chicken in a large plastic ziplock or vacpac bag as it's easier to turn to ensure even brining.

....

····· Cook ·········· Pair ·····

Cook	Pair
Chimay Blue – Belgium	Cromarty Brewing Red Rocker – UK
Unibroue Maudite – Canada	Ska Pinstripe Red Ale – USA
La Trappe Dubbel – Netherlands	Two Birds Sunset – Australia
Gordon's Scotch Ale – Belgium	Bear Republic Red Rocket – USA
Brouwerij Kees Wee Heavy – Netherlands	Magic Rock Rapture – UK

Lamb, Haggis & Seaweed Kebab with Quick-pickled Swede

Serves 4

Ingredients

For the kebab:

400 g (14 oz) minced (ground) lamb (around 20% fat)

200 g (7 oz) haggis, skinned and chopped into 2 cm (¾ in) cubes*

60 g (2 oz) laverbread (use the other half for/or from Moules à la Biere recipe on page 82)

100 ml (3½ fl oz/scant ½ cup) honey ale (specifically braggot if you can get it)

2 tablespoons ras el hanout

1 tablespoon ground cumin

1 tablespoon ground coriander

2–4 tablespoons harissa

2 teaspoons fine sea salt

groundnut, grapeseed or other neutral oil

if you can't get haggis then use 25 g (1 oz) finely chopped chicken livers to 150 g (5 oz) plain sausage meat, season with 2 teaspoons of salt and 1 tablespoon of ground black pepper

For the quick-pickled swede:

1 tablespoon fine sea salt

1½ teaspoons caster (superfine) sugar

20 ml (¾ fl oz/generous 1 tablespoon) hot water

330 ml (11¼ fl oz/1⅓ cups) well-chilled plain Berliner weisse

50 ml (1¾ fl oz/scant ¼ cup) white wine vinegar

200 g (7 oz) swede, peeled and cut into 2 cm- (¾ in-) thick slices

1 teaspoon dried wakame seaweed

cold water, if needed, to top up

To assemble:

shop-bought flatbread (or Flexible Flatbread, page 50)

iceberg lettuce, finely shredded

Tzatziki (page 75)

chilli sauce of choice

I would like to state for the record that I was not drunk when I came up with this recipe; it was conjured up on Burn's Night for a friend who was convalescing after an operation, and whose husband is Welsh, which is where the braggot (a traditionally Welsh honey beer) and laverbread (a Welsh seaweed product) come in. Basically, it's a Celtic crossover via a post-pub special, which is apt as the friends I mention own a few hostelries themselves.

Method

First prepare the pickled swede. Put the salt and sugar in a large non-metallic bowl, add the hot water and stir vigorously to dissolve.

Add the beer and vinegar, then the swede and wakame. Add enough cold water, if needed, to cover the vegetables, then refrigerate for no longer than 4 hours before using.

Meanwhile, to make the kebab, add the minced lamb to a large metal mixing bowl. Add the remaining ingredients, except the oil, and using your hands, squish it all together, being careful not to break up the haggis too much. Sometimes it is best to do this process in stages to make the mixture more manageable.

Once everything is combined, wash your hands and then lightly oil them.

Put a dry frying pan (skillet) on a medium heat.

Form your mixture into 4 kebabs and place them in your hot frying pan. They should hiss satisfyingly as they hit the surface.

Cook slowly on each side, brushing the surface of the kebab with a little more oil, if necessary, until done.

Wrap the kebab into your flatbreads with your pickled swede, lettuce, tzatziki, chilli sauce, and whatever ever else you may fancy!

Cook ·········· Pair

Two Sisters Brewing Brigid's Ale – Ireland

Brasserie Lefebvre Barbãr – Belgium

Fuller's Honey Dew – UK

Sleemans Honey Brown – Canada

Mata Manuka Ale – New Zealand

Camden Hells – UK

Cigar City Tampa-Style Lager – USA

Thornbridge Lukas – UK

Schlenkerla Helles – Germany

Moo Brew Beer Can – Australia

··· Cook ··········· : ··········· Pair ···

Cook	Pair
Rudgate Ruby Mild – UK	Fuller's ESB – UK
NOLA Brown Ale – USA	3 Floyds Lord Rear Admiral – USA
Moorhouse's Black Cat – UK	Hook Norton Old Hooky – UK
Tooheys Old – Australia	Theakston's Old Peculier – UK
Timothy Taylor's Dark Mild – UK	Dougall's Leyenda – Spain

Ben's Welcome Home Hotpot
Serves 6

Ingredients

2 tablespoon oil

500 g (1 lb 2 oz) black pudding, skin removed, cut into bite-sized chunks

1 kg (2 lb 4 oz) neck of lamb, chopped into bite-sized pieces

4 onions, sliced into half-moons, 1 cm (½ in) thick

50 g (2 oz) butter, cut into small cubes, plus extra for greasing

1 kg (2 lb 4 oz) potatoes, peeled and cut into slices about 2 cm (¾ in) thick

4 lambs' kidneys, cored, sinew removed and cut into 2 cm (¾ in) cubes

steamed carrots and peas, to serve

For the gravy:

200 ml (7 fl oz/scant 1 cup) English-style dark mild★

1 tablespoon dried thyme

120 ml (4 fl oz/½ cup) lamb stock (feel free to use a stock cube if you can't find anything else/don't want to make it)

2 tablespoons groundnut, grapeseed or other neutral oil

2 tablespoons Worcestershire sauce

1 tablespoon English mustard

1 tablespoon red miso paste (miso paste makes gravies so much better!)

salt and freshly ground black pepper

★ historically mild meant beer to be drunk fresh as it was only mildly hopped

My other half doesn't spend much time in the kitchen, not by choice I hasten to add, I'm just a bit territorial*; but when I was away on a long trip recently he decided to turn his hand to a delicious Lancashire hotpot and it was exactly what I needed to greet me after a 20-hour journey.

I was so smitten that I suggested we work on a very slight beer variation together, and when I mused about what beer style should go in, he immediately said 'mild' and I knew straight away he was right. So, even if you don't believe in any other recipe in the book, you at least know that this one's had the seal of approval from the long-suffering Mr Melissa.

You'll need a 20 cm (8 in) casserole dish with a lid for this. *Ok, I'll admit it, I'm a nightmare control freak in the kitchen who likes to do all the cooking…

Method

Preheat the oven to 180°C (350°F/Gas 4) and put the lid for your casserole dish in the oven.

First, prepare the gravy. Put the beer, thyme and stock in a saucepan over a medium heat. Simmer to reduce by one-third and thicken slightly.

Meanwhile, heat a large frying pan (skillet) over a high heat and quickly fry the black pudding with 1 tablespoon of the oil then set aside.

Wipe the pan clean and return to the heat, add the remaining oil and brown the lamb neck.

Turn the heat down and push the meat to one side of the pan. Add the onions and fry for about 10 minutes until softened, then mix together with the meat.

Stir in the Worcestershire sauce, mustard and miso into the beer-stock mix. Check the seasoning, adding salt and pepper if required.

Butter the inside of the casserole dish and line the base with a layer of potatoes.

Put the lamb, onions and black pudding mixture and kidneys on top and fill two thirds of the pot with your reduced gravy (using any remaining beer to make up the volume if needed). Finish with a nicely arranged layer of potatoes.

Dot the potatoes with butter, take the hot casserole lid from the oven (using a cloth or oven gloves) and place on the casserole dish. Put on the middle shelf of the oven, turning it down to 160°C (325°F/Gas 3) as you close the door. Cook for 25 minutes.

Remove the lid and cook for another 20 minutes until the potatoes are golden and crispy.

Take out of the oven and allow to rest for 10 minutes. Serve with carrots and peas.

Chilli con Carne

Serves 8–10

Ingredients

500 ml (17 fl oz/2 cups) German-style hefeweizen

1 large chipotle chilli

3 ancho chillies

3 cascabel chillies

100 g (3½ oz) bacon grease, lard or beef dripping or 100 ml (3½ oz/scant ½ cup) groundnut, grapeseed or other neutral oil

1 kg (2 lb 4 oz) beef shin meat or braising steak, cut into 2.5 cm (1 in) cubes

500 g (1 lb 2 oz) pork shoulder, cut into 2.5 cm (1 in) cubes

5 white or yellow onions, diced (or 500–550 g/1 lb 2 oz–1 lb 4 oz pre-chopped frozen onions)

8 large garlic cloves, pounded to a paste (or 3 tablespoons pre-chopped frozen garlic)

6 tablespoons cumin seeds, toasted, put into a spice grinder with a pinch of coarse sea salt and blitzed

4 tablespoons dried Mexican oregano

3 fresh bay leaves

1 stick Ceylon cinnamon

1 tablespoon ground coriander

1 litre (34 fl oz/4 cups) creamed tomato or passata (sieved tomatoes)

100 g (3½ oz) tomato purée (paste)

330 ml (11¼ fl oz/1⅓ cups) coffee milk stout

2 large, fresh green jalapeño chillies, stems removed

1 fresh Scotch bonnet, stem removed (optional)

1 tablespoon chipotle chilli (hot pepper) flakes

1 tablespoon ancho chilli flakes

1 tablespoon red chilli (hot pepper) flakes

2 × 400 g (14 oz) tins of beans of choice (I used black and black eyed beans), drained and rinced

4 squares of dark chocolate with 80% cocoa solids

sea salt and freshly ground black pepper

To serve, aka 'fixins':

500 g (1 lb 2 oz) mature Cheddar, grated

300 ml (10 fl oz/1¼ cups) sour cream

large bunch of chives, very finely chopped

crusty baguette, slathered in salted butter

I first used this spice, chocolate and beer mix for the chilli I served at my 40th birthday party. I had 50 guests and had made enough for 80 … it took exactly half an hour for my friends and family to decimate it, leaving me to scrape a quarter bowl for myself, and even then I had to fight my beloved nephew, Josh, for it.

I am erring away from kidney beans in this because I don't like them very much, but feel free to include them or any other favoured bean. And, finally, you will need a BIG pot or slow cooker for this.

Mexican and Mediterranean oregano are botanically different. The former comes from the *Lippia* family and the latter from the *Origanum* family meaning they do have genuinely different flavours.

Ceylon cinnamon is significantly more savoury and less aggressive than the sweeter, more assertive cassia cinnamon that we're more used to using for baking and works better in savoury dishes. If you find it hard to buy then use half a stick of the cassia one.

Cook ·········· Pair

Cook	Pair
Sierra Nevada Kellerweis – USA	Hacker-Pschorr Weisse Dark – Germany
COEDO Shiro – Japan	Meantime London Porter – UK
Bohemia 14 Weiss – Brazil	Zywiec Porter – Poland
Saint Arnold Weedwacker – USA	Anchor Porter – USA
4 Pines Hefeweizen – Australia	Carnegie Stark Porter – Sweden

Method

Preheat the oven to 120°C (250°F/Gas ½).

Warm the hefeweizen gently in a pan. When it's just beginning to steam slightly, turn off the heat and add the chipotle, ancho and cascabel chillies. Set aside and leave to soften.

Heat your chosen fat in a large ovenproof cooking pot over a high heat until it shimmers, then lightly brown off the meat, in batches, refreshing the amount of oil and allowing it to heat up properly between batches. Season to taste, spoon the cooked meat into a large bowl and set to one side.

In the residual fat from the last batch of meat, gently fry the onions over a low heat for 10–15 minutes until light brown in colour, stirring every minute or so. Add the garlic and cook for another few minutes, stirring gently.

Return the brewed meat to the pot with the cumin, oregano, bay leaves, cinnamon, coriander, passata, tomato purée and coffee milk stout and simmer.

Meanwhile, remove the soaked chillies from the beer (reserve the liquid), take off their stems, and place in a blender, along with the jalapeños and the Scotch bonnet. Blitz them up into a paste, then, with caution (as it's hot!), scrape into the simmering meat pot.

Add the remaining chilli flakes (see note), then pour the reserved beer liquid into the pot and top up with a little water if necessary. Put the lid on and place in oven for 4 hours.

Add the beans then cook for another 30–90 minutes, with the lid off, depending on the tenderness of the meat.

Remove the pot from the oven, stir in half the chocolate and test for salt – it's best to under-season it a little for two reasons: firstly the cheese will bring some salt and also when you reheat it, the liquid will reduce further.

Put the 'fixins' on the table and let everyone dig in and personalise with as much or as little of the cheese, sour cream and chives as they like. Enjoy!

113

SOME EFFORT

··········
NOTE: If you're worried about the heat, add ½ tablespoon of each of the flakes first and then try the liquid after about an hour's cooking. If it's not hot enough, increase to taste.
··········

Spanish-style Rabbit with Honey Beer
Serves 2

Ingredients

1 rabbit, portioned but left on the bone (try and buy wild rabbit – it's hard to source ethically farmed rabbit, which is also quite bland)

fine sea salt, to season

good-quality extra-virgin olive oil, to fry

2 onions, diced

4 garlic cloves, pounded to a paste with a little salt

1 tablespoon plain (all-purpose) flour

2 teaspoons ground almonds

500 ml (17 fl oz/2 cups) sweet honey beer (I used Fuller's Honey Dew)

400 g (14 oz) tin of cherry tomatoes, drained of liquid (reserve the liquid in the freezer for another dish)

2 large sprigs of oregano or marjoram

1 bay leaf

1 teaspoon chilli (hot pepper) flakes (optional)

freshly ground black pepper

chopped parsley and orange wedges, to serve

This was one of the earliest recipes I can remember making for my other half more years ago than I care to remember. It seemed so daunting at the time because I knew from childhood how very tough over-cooked rabbit is (not yours Mum, it was great!).

I like to serve this on a bed of wilted spinach and sautéed potatoes but you could always go with a Spanish-inspired side and make the fun and slightly different Patatas Bravas Pots (opposite).

This is the only recipe where I'll break my 'don't bother to cook with extra-virgin olive oil' rule because you don't cook on a high enough heat to break it down and it adds so much to the finished dish.

Method

Begin by seasoning the rabbit with salt. Put a large frying pan (skillet) on a medium-high heat, add a good 2 cm (¾ in) of olive oil and allow to gently heat. Gently brown the rabbit on all sides, then remove from the pan and set aside.

Turn the heat down to medium-low, add the onions and fry for about 5 minutes until they are translucent. Add the garlic and continue to fry for another 5 minutes or until the garlic starts to smell sweet.

Sprinkle in the flour, a pinch of salt and the almonds, and stir, for a few minutes until you can smell a light nuttiness.

Add two-thirds of the bottle of beer along with the tomatoes, herbs and chilli, reduce the heat to medium-low and simmer gently for 3 minutes.

Turn the heat down to low, return the rabbit to the pan and simmer gently for 25–30 minutes. (The finished internal temperature should be 71°C/160°F, meaning you can take it off the heat at about 69°C /156°F.) Add a little more beer if the sauce gets too dry, and check for seasoning, adding a fresh grind of black pepper as you do.

Just before serving, sprinkle the rabbit with chopped parsley and serve with orange wedges.

Cook

Fuller's Honey Dew – UK

Matilda Bay Beez Neez – Australia

Benford Brewing Irish Honey Ale – USA

Brasserie Lefebvre Barbār – Belgium

Hiver Honey Beer Pale – UK

Pair

Whistler Bear Paw Lager – Canada

Rogue Honey Kolsch – USA

Olde Hansa Crafty Monk Dark Honey – Estonia

Hiver Honey Beer Dark – UK

Dogfish Head Midas Touch – USA

Recipe photo overleaf

Patatas Bravas Pots
Serves 2

Ingredients

2 large baking potatoes, between 800 g–1 kg (1 lb 12 oz–3 lb 6 oz) each and as flat as possible

fine sea salt

3 tablespoons olive oil (about 6 cm/ 2½ in), to fry

For the sauce:

This will make a bit more than is needed but it can be used as pizza base, a pasta sauce or frozen to use on more patatas bravas.

½ tablespoon olive oil

2 yellow onions, finely chopped

4 garlic cloves, pounded to a paste with a little salt

400 g (14 oz) tin of cherry tomatoes

200 ml (7 fl oz/scant 1 cup) hefeweizen

1 tablespoon sundried tomato purée (paste)

2 teaspoons sweet smoked paprika

1 teaspoon hot smoked paprika

1 teaspoon chilli (hot pepper) flakes

½ teaspoon caster (superfine) sugar

extra-virgin olive oil, to drizzle

chopped parsley leaves, to garnish

Cook

Birra Tarì Vicerè – Italy

Sierra Nevada Kellerweis – USA

COEDO Shiro – Japan

Rothaus Hefeweizen – Germany

Bohemia 14 Weiss – Brazil

Pair

Thornbridge Kill Your Darlings – UK

Moa Noir – New Zealand

Anspach & Hobday Table Porter – UK

Shiner Bohemian Black – USA

Xingu Black Beer – Brazil

This recipe reminds me of the fun of taking my niece and nephew to a West London tapas bar where they serve their patatas bravas in a similar fashion and my niece, in particular, absolutely loved them and the first time I attempted the recipe we cooked them together, so this one is for my beloved Kate.

Method

Peel and halve the potatoes, then shape each half into an 8 × 8 × 10 cm (3¼ × 3¼ × 4 in) cuboid (see photo overleaf). Keep the offcuts for another use (see note).

Fill a steamer with water and add 1 tablespoon of fine sea salt and set to the boil. Put the cubed potatoes in the steamer basket and cook for 10 minutes. Leave the cubes to sit over the remaining hot water until they cool. Place in the fridge for at least an hour.

Stand the potatoes with the longest side facing you and, using an apple corer, take out the middles, making sure you leave 2 cm (¾ in) at the bottom.

Heat the olive oil in a saucepan, just large enough to fit the potatoes in on their sides, over a medium-high heat. When the pan is too hot for you to hold your hand over for more than a few seconds, gently lower in the potatoes and leave to cook until golden brown.

Remove the potatoes from the pan with tongs, pouring out any oil from the centres, and place on some paper towel in an ovenproof dish. Set aside.

To make the sauce, heat the oil over a medium-low heat and fry the onions for about 5 minutes until translucent. Add the garlic and cook for a further 5 minutes until it smells sweet.

Add the other ingredients, apart from the extra-virgin olive oil and parsley, and simmer over a low heat for 30 minutes until reduced to a thick, but still spoonable, sauce. Leave to cool until just warm.

Preheat the oven to 180°C (350°F/Gas 4).

Put the potato pots on a roasting tray (pan) and fill them with the spicy tomato sauce (I find a sauce bottle with the spout cut off very useful for this). Bake in the hot oven for 15 minutes.

Once ready to serve, drizzle over some extra-virgin olive oil and sprinkle with parsley.

....

NOTE: You can cook the offcuts in the water that's used to steam the potatoes. Remove after 10 minutes, drain, cool and store in the freezer for another day.

You may be able to make more than 4 bravas pots – it all depends on the shape of your potatoes!

....

SOME EFFORT

Recipe photo overleaf

Gingery Ham
Serves 6

Ingredients

1.5 kg (3 lb 5 oz) unsmoked gammon joint

2 carrots, whole or roughly chopped

2 celery sticks, whole or roughly chopped

1 white onion, roughly chopped

1 garlic bulbs, cut in half crossways

2 dried chillies or 1 tablespoon chilli (hot pepper) flakes

1 thumb-sized piece of fresh ginger root, peeled and roughly chopped

2 tablespoons fennel seeds

1 tablespoon lampung or ordinary black peppercorns

1 bay leaf

1 tablespoon salt

500 ml (17 fl oz/2 cups) alcoholic ginger beer

500 ml (17 fl oz/2 cups) beer with ginger in it

330 ml (11¼ fl oz/1⅓ cups) can fiery ginger beer

2 tablespoons cornflour (cornstarch), mixed to a paste with 1 tablespoon red miso paste and some cooking liquor

For the glaze:

2 each of green and black cardamom pods

5 tablespoons maple syrup

2 tablespoons English mustard powder

1 tablespoon soft brown sugar

2 teaspoons unsalted butter

Like pretty much everyone who has clapped eyes on Nigella Lawson's iconic cola ham, I decided to give it a go around Christmas one year but I ran into a small problem: I'd forgotten to buy any cola. What I did have, however, was lots of alcoholic drinks with ginger and some fiery ginger beer in the house, so I decided to use those instead and, hey presto, it worked. My best friend from university, Gillian Robson, swears by it, but she's Scottish, so that's nothing unusual…

....

NOTE: I've already talked low and slow cooking elsewhere in the book, but the added bonus here is ginger contains powerful enzymes that help tenderise the meat, but they die above 37.5°C (99°F), which is why I heat the liquid really slowly to give them a bit of time to act.

....

Method

Place the gammon in a large saucepan, cover with cold water, put on the heat and bring to just below boiling point. Simmer for 10 minutes. Strain and discard the water.

Put the gammon back in the pan with the remaining ingredients, except the cornflour, then top up with cold water to cover the joint. Put over a very low heat and allow to warm up until the liquid is just quivering. Simmer very gently for 3 hours or until the gammon is completely tender.

Allow to cool in the cooking liquor, then lift the ham out, reserving the liquid.

Half an hour before you're ready to serve, preheat the oven to 200°C (400°F/Gas 6).

Carefully remove the skin and score the fat in a diamond pattern. Place the meat on a trivet in a roasting tray (pan) and roast in the oven for 10 minutes so the fat starts to crisp slightly.

Meanwhile prepare the glaze. Remove the seeds from the cardamom pods and crush to a powder. Put in a saucepan with the rest of the glaze ingredients, and simmer over a low heat, stirring occasionally until everything melts together.

Remove the ham from the oven, turn the heat down to 180°C (350°F/Gas 4) and lift the ham, still on the trivet, out of the tray.

For the gravy, pour 500 g (1 lb 2 oz) of the reserved cooking liquor into the base of the roasting tray to come halfway up (see tip), then stir in the cornflour mixture.

Put the ham on the trivet back in the roasting tray. Glaze the top liberally and the sides lightly, then put it back in the oven for 10 minutes. Remove and glaze every 10 minutes for 30–40 minutes, making sure it doesn't burn and that the gravy doesn't dry out.

Rest the meat on the board for at least 15 minutes but keep the cooking juices in the pan warm in the oven.

Just before serving, pour the roasting tray gravy into a warmed gravy jug and take the meat to the table for people to admire.

....

TIP: Any leftover cooking liquor makes an excellent stock base, I love using it for pea and ham soup or curries, just be aware it is generally a bit salty.

....

Cook

The pairings for this depend entirely on how you are serving it up, so I'm going to leave you to experiment for yourself with those! I also just want to stop and say, sometimes beers brewed with ginger can be tough to find, so you can substitute with a Belgian wheat beer and 2 tablespoons of syrup from preserved ginger.

St Austell Sayzon – UK

Left Hand Good JúJu – USA

Hitachino Nest Real Ginger Brew – Japan

Hollow's & Fentiman's Alcoholic Ginger Beer – UK

Boulevard Lemon & Ginger Radler – USA

Lamb Boulangère
Serves 6–8

Ingredients

2.25–2.5 kg (5 lb 8 oz–5 lb 10 oz) bone-in lamb shoulder

4 tablespoons anchovy paste (if you can't find the paste, pound 20–30 preserved anchovies to a paste in a pestle and mortar)

10 large sprigs of lemon or ordinary thyme, leaves picked and finely chopped

1.5 kg (3 lb 5 oz) waxy potatoes

2 red onions

1 large garlic bulb, cloves lightly crushed

2 teaspoons fine sea salt

2 teaspoons freshly ground black pepper

330 ml (11¼ fl oz/1⅓ cups) spruce or pine beer

500 ml (17 fl oz/2 cups) chicken or lamb stock (or however much will fit, reserve the rest)

For the gravy:

1 tablespoon cornflour (cornstarch)

1 tablespoon dark soy sauce

1 tablespoon red miso paste

This is one of my go-to lazy Sunday roast recipes. As I've mentioned before, I'm not renowned for my patience and normally for a dish like this you'd be exhorted to poke little holes in the lamb skin and stick anchovies, herbs and slivers of garlic in them – but it's such a lot of fuss, so I've devised a simpler and, pleasingly, more efficient way to infuse these flavours into your meat.

Two quick notes on this: firstly, buy a cheap mandoline – it's an invaluable kitchen tool, but always use the guard. Don't argue with me! Cutting yourself on a mandoline blade is a sickening feeling that you'll never forget – trust me. Second, you will need a BIG roasting dish and some turkey foil or a large roasting tray (pan) with a lid.

Cook ⸱⸱⸱⸱⸱ Pair

Spruce, juniper and pine beers can often be seasonal, so feel free to substitute a tripel, gently heated for a few minutes with some rosemary or pine/spruce tips and left to stand for 10 minutes.

Williams Bros Alba – UK

Finlandia Sahti – Finland

Pihtla Beer – Estonia

Pinta Koniec Świata – Poland

Rogue Yellow Snow Pilsner – USA

Tripel Karmeliet – Belgium

Unibroue La Fin du Monde – Canada

Westmalle Tripel – Belgium

Wäls Trippel – Brazil

St Austell Bad Habit – UK

Recipe method overleaf

Preheat the oven to 140°C (275°F/Gas 1).

Turn the lamb shoulder skin-side down and make 3 cm- (1¼ in-) deep incisions to create a large diamond grid pattern in the flesh. Take the anchovy paste and a tablespoon of the thyme leaves, mix them together and rub them into the incisions. Set aside.

Into the base of the roasting tray (pan), slice two-thirds of the potatoes and all the onions, evenly scatter over the garlic cloves and the remaining thyme leaves, season with half the salt and the pepper. Mix together with your hands, breaking the onions up into rings as you go.

Roughly smooth out the top of the potato mixture, add the beer and the chicken or lamb stock, then, with the remaining potatoes, make two neat overlapping rings, one inside the other on the top around the outside.

Put the lamb shoulder, flesh-side down, in the middle of the potatoes and very lightly score the top in a smaller diamond grid pattern, literally just scratching the surface with the knife. Season with the remaining salt and pepper.

Put the lid/foil on and pop in the oven for 30 minutes.

Turn the heat down to 120°C (250°F/Gas ½) and cook for 5–6 hours. When the lamb is ready, you will be able to pull the shoulder bone out with little or no resistance.

At that point, lift the lamb out very carefully and place on a large plate, cover with kitchen foil and pop back in the oven.

Carefully pour off any excess roasting juices from the potatoes (it's helpful to have an extra pair of hands for this if you can) into a large saucepan.

Turn the oven up to 200°C (400°F/Gas 6), take the lamb out and put the potatoes back in. Leave the lamb somewhere warmish to rest.

To make the gravy, mix the cornflour, soy and miso in a small bowl, add a ladle of the cooking juices and whisk together with a fork.

Add this mixture to any juices in the saucepan and allow to bubble gently over a low heat and reduce to your desired gravy consistency.

When the potatoes are browned, turn the oven off, crack open the door slightly, and return the lamb to the middle of the dish. Put your serving plates in to warm.

Cook whatever vegetables you require and bring everything to the table to serve.

Coconut Beer Rendang
Serves 6

Growing up near the cultural melting pot that is Slough (just outside London), where the heady smell of spice in the air is part of its DNA, there's something about walking into my home, with the smell of rendang heavy in the air, that I find tremendously comforting.

Traditionally it's cooked on a hob or over an open flame but that does requires a tremendous amount of attention, so I favour cooking it in either the oven or a slow cooker on low. This recipe serves six but it can be easily halved or freezes well.

Ingredients

For the meat:

groundnut, grapeseed or other neutral oil

1 kg (2 lb 4 oz) beef shin/stewing steak), cut into 4 cm (1½ in) chunks

fine sea salt

For the spice paste:

100 g (3½ oz/1¼ cups) desiccated coconut, carefully dry toasted in a pan until a caramel brown

6 macadamia nuts (or 4 candlenuts)

1 large garlic bulb, separated into cloves

4 large red finger chillies, roughly chopped

2 red Thai bird's eye chillies or other hot chilli (optional)

250 g (9 oz) onions, roughly chopped

50 g (2 oz) fresh ginger root, peeled and roughly chopped

50 g (2 oz) galangal, skinned and roughly chopped (use 100 g/3½ oz fresh ginger if unavailable)

50 g (2 oz) fresh turmeric, roughly chopped (or 20 g/¾ oz ground turmeric)

2 teaspoons of ground coriander

2 teaspoons of ground cumin

seeds from 6 green cardamoms pods and 2 black cardamom pods

2 teaspoons salt

1 tablespoon groundnut oil

50 ml (1¾ fl oz/scant ¼ cup) coconut beer (reserve the rest for cooking)

For the coconut base:

300 g (10½ oz) creamed coconut, roughly chopped

300 ml (10 fl oz/1¼ cups) coconut milk

4 fresh lemongrass stalks, outer sheath removed and tender stalk bruised

6 fresh kaffir lime leaves, bruised (use dried if fresh is unavailable)

1 tablespoon tamarind paste

Method

Heat the oven to 120°C (250°F/Gas 1) or prepare your slow cooker.

Blitz all the spice paste ingredients in a food processor, adding a little more beer to get it going if necessary.

Put a large frying pan (skillet) on a medium-high heat with a couple of tablespoons of groundnut oil. Brown the meat in batches. Turn up the heat, if necessary, but do not crowd the pan or it will just stew. Season lightly with small pinches of fine sea salt for each batch as you fry.

Using the same pan without cleaning it (assuming there's no burnt matter in there, if so wipe clean with paper towels) add 1 tablespoon of oil and, over a low heat, gently fry the spice paste for 5–8 minutes until it goes slightly deeper in colour.

Add the meat, creamed coconut, coconut milk, lemongrass, kaffir lime leaves and the rest of the coconut beer into the spice paste. Mix well and then put in an oven-proof dish or slow cooker.

Cook on low for 4–6 hours until thick and the meat is totally tender. Just before serving stir in the tamarind paste and check the seasoning.

Cook ··········· Pair ·······

Cook	Pair
Cervejaria Narcose Mora Mora – Brazil	Chimay Blue – Belgium
Neptune On the Bounty – UK	Bell's Hell Hath No Fury – USA
Maui Brewing Coconut Hiwa Porter – USA	La Trappe Dubbel – Netherlands
Basqueland Brewing Project Coco Chango – Spain	Savour Dubbel – UK
Evil Twin Even More Coco Jesus – USA	TicketyBrew Dubbel – UK

Citrusy Posset
Serves 4

Ingredients

finely grated zest and juice of 2 small or 1 very large unwaxed lemon (Amalfi if you can)

finely grated zest and juice of 1 unwaxed lime

50 g (2 oz) citrus session IPA or pale ale

100 g (3½ oz/1⅔ cups) golden caster (superfine) sugar

a pinch of fine sea salt

425 ml (15 fl oz/generous 1⅔ cups) extra thick double (heavy) cream

For the topping:

25 g (1 oz) caster (superfine) sugar

25 g (1 oz) water

25 g (1 oz) citrus session IPA/pale ale/IPA

1 lemongrass stalk, smashed

1 thumb-sized piece of fresh ginger root, peeled and sliced (about 1 cm/½ in thick)

sea salt flakes, to decorate

Posset is something we know better as a dessert these days, but it actually started life as a drink, and it is said that a well-made posset had three different layers.

The uppermost, known as 'the grace' was a snowy foam or aereated crust. In the middle was a smooth, spicy custard and at the bottom a pungent alcoholic liquid. The grace and the custard were enthusiastically consumed as 'spoonmeat' and the sack-rich liquid below drunk through the 'pipe' or spout of the posset pot.'

Method

First measure out 15 g (½ oz) of the lemon and lime zest for the posset. Reserve any extra for the topping.

Place the beer, citrus juice, measured zest, sugar and a small pinch of salt in a saucepan. Slowly heat until the sugar dissolves and the liquid is viscous, coating the back of a spoon easily.

In a separate pan, gently heat the cream until it's just about to boil, stir, then pour in the syrup and mix well. Pass through a fine sieve into a small heatproof jug, tap lightly on the side to drive off any bubbles.

Pour into 4 ramekins (custard cups) and use the corner of a piece of paper towel to absorb any bubbles on the surface. Allow to cool, then refrigerate.

To make the topping, gently heat the sugar, water, beer, lemongrass, ginger and any remaining lemon and lime zest in a pan and simmer softly to reduce until the mixture will thickly coat the back of a spoon.

Once the syrup is nice and sticky, pass through a sieve into a jug, allow to cool in fridge with the posset for an hour.

Take the chilled possets and topping out of the fridge at least half an hour before serving, to let come to room temperature.

Pour the topping over the possets, again using a paper towel to catch any bubbles, and sprinkle over some sea salt flakes to serve.

Cook ……… Pair

Any of the beers you're using to make this dessert will go well with it but I like the slight astringency of the suggested pairings. But I don't have a huge sweet tooth.

Green Flash Tangerine Soul Style IPA – USA

Fourpure Juicebox IPA – UK

Captain Lawrence Effortless Grapefruit IPA – USA

Kees Pink Grapefruit – Netherlands

Baird Beer Temple Garden Yuzu – Japan

Marble Brewery Earl Grey – UK

Yeastie Boys Gunnamatta – New Zealand

Siren Craft Brew Yu Lu – UK

Brasserie Licorne Kasteel Cru – France

Yellow Belly Citra Pale Ale – Ireland

Grado Plato Wiezentea – Italy

Magnificent Malt Loaf

Makes a 900 g (2 lb) loaf

Ingredients

75 ml (2½ fl oz/5 tablespoons) strong, cold black tea

75 ml (2½ fl oz/5 tablespoons) mild*, plus 25 g (1 oz), to finish

150 g (5 oz/scant 1¼ cups) raisins

150 g (5 oz/scant 1¼ cups) dried prunes, chopped into raisin-sized chunks

unsalted butter, for greasing

175 g (6 oz) malt extract, plus 4 tablespoons extra for finishing

85 g (3 oz/½ cup) dark muscovado sugar (this is a must, do not substitute)

2 large eggs, beaten

100 g (3½ oz/heaped ¾ cup) wholemeal flour

150 g (5 oz/scant 1¼ cups) plain (all-purpose) or spelt flour

1 teaspoon bicarbonate of soda (baking soda)

2½ teaspoons baking powder

★ just to be clear here, mild refers to the type of beer not the flavour

I love malt loaf. It's something that was a feature of my childhood because either my Mum had made it or because my friends' Mums had or it was from a yellow packet – whichever way it came, it was always handed to me toasted and with lashings of salted butter on it.

My heart doesn't want to give you a beer pairing for this, because I think it should be enjoyed for the innocent treat it is so, just like fish and chips, Granddad Biscuits (page 87) and any form of breakfast, I'm not going to directly suggest a pairing, I'm just going to mention that the mild you cooked it with wouldn't be terrible on the side.

Method

In a saucepan, gently heat the tea and mild until bubbles just start to break the surface. Add the dried fruit, remove the pan from the heat and leave to stand for 15 minutes.

Preheat the oven to 150°C (300°F/Gas 1), making sure the shelf is in the middle. Grease and line a 900 g (2 lb) loaf tin (pan) or baking dish with an oversized piece of lightly dampened and scrunched baking parchment.

Stir the malt extract and sugar into the beer and fruit mixture until the sugar is fully dissolved. Still stirring, add the beaten eggs.

In a separate bowl, mix together the flours, bicarbonate of soda and baking powder. Add the liquid ingredients to the dry ingredients, stirring vigorously until well blended, then leave to stand for 15 minutes.

Pour the mixture into the prepared loaf pan and bake on the middle shelf of the oven for 50 minutes, or until a skewer inserted in the middle comes out clean. It's likely to look a bit collapsed, but don't worry, it's part of the character.

Take the loaf out of the oven and leave to cool in its pan on a wire cooling rack. Leave for 10 minutes.

While the cake is still cooling, warm the finishing malt extract and extra malt together in a saucepan over a low heat. Don't allow it to boil. Remove from the heat.

Poke holes into your loaf with a skewer and brush the cake liberally with the malt and beer mix, allowing each application to seep into the holes. Leave to cool.

Lift the cake out of the tin, still in its baking parchment, wrap it in more baking parchment and then tightly in cling film (plastic wrap). If you can manage it, leave in a cool, dark place for at least 3 days, before enjoying.

Cook

Hillside Over the Hill Mild – UK

Rudgate Ruby Mild – UK

NOLA Brown Ale – USA

Moorhouse's Black Cat – UK

Tooheys Old – Australia

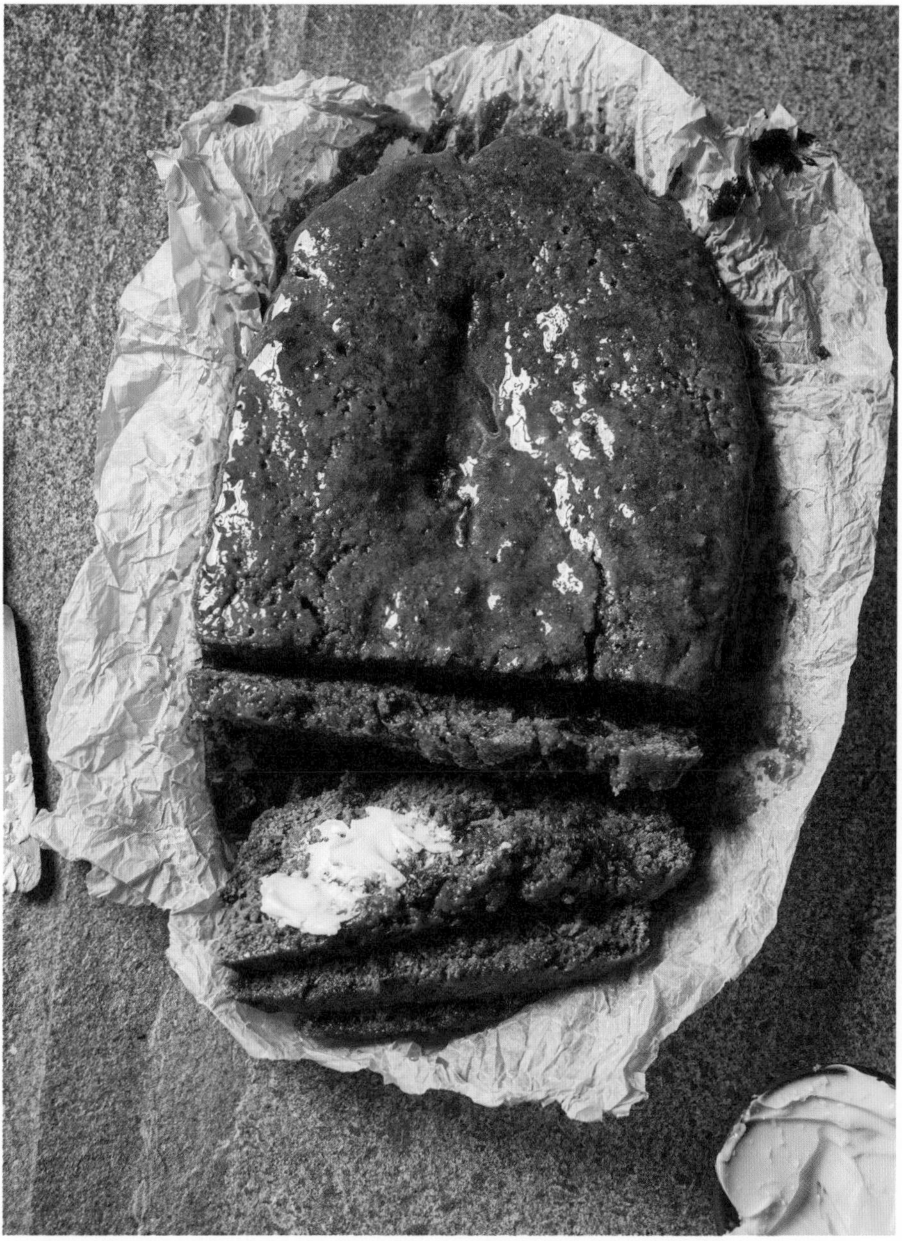

Apple Crumble Beer Pie with Mild Custard

Serves 6

Ingredients

1 kg (2 lb 4 oz) cooking apples such as Bramleys

100 ml (3½ oz/scant ½ cup) apple or pumpkin beer

1 tablespoon plain (all-purpose) flour, plus extra for dusting

For the crumble topping:

200 g (7 oz) plain (all-purpose) flour

100 g (3½ oz/1 cup) rolled oats

150 g (5 oz) unsalted butter, plus extra for greasing

200 g (7 oz/1 cup) demerara sugar

Ahhh, crumble, it's something that nowhere in the world does as well as we do in the UK – sorry, Americans, but it's true. This is another one of those recipes you can play around with. You can use pears, blackberries, rhubarb – anything that has that little bite of acidity and warm winter flavours will work well here.

Method

Heat the oven to 180°C (350°F/Gas 4). Grease and flour a 20 cm (8 in) pie pan.

Peel, core and slice the apples. Put them in a pan with the beer and then put on a low heat for 7 minutes until the outsides are just getting soft. Gently stir in the flour, then allow to cool a little.

Make the crumble topping by adding all the crumble topping ingredients to a food processor and gently pulsing until the mixture resembles fat breadcrumbs.

Spoon the apples into the pie pan and sprinkle the crumble mixtyre over the top. Bake for about 30–40 minutes until the crumble is golden brown.

Mild Custard

Serves 6

Ingredients

200 ml (7 fl oz/scant 1 cup) double (heavy) cream

700 ml (24 fl oz/scant 3 cups) whole (full-fat) milk

3 tablespoons cornflour (cornstarch)

2 tablespoons mild beer*

185 g (6½ oz/generous ¾ cup) caster (superfine) sugar

1 tablespoon maple syrup

1 teaspoon vanilla bean paste

4 large egg yolks (you can freeze the whites for use in meringues on page 181)

just to be clear here, mild refers to the type of beer not the flavour

Method

Place the cream and milk in a saucepan over a low heat and gently bring to just below boiling point.

Meanwhile, in a large bowl, blend the cornflour to a paste with the beer, then whisk in the sugar, maple syrup and vanilla. Whisk in the egg yolks.

Slowly add the warm cream mixture to the egg and sugar mixture, whisking briskly.

Return the mixture to the saucepan and warm slowly, stirring constantly with a wooden spoon for about 5 minutes until the custard sticks well to the back of it.

Put a circle of baking parchment on top to stop a skin forming or pour straight into a heatproof jug and serve over your crumble pie!

⋯ Cook ⋯⋯⋯⋯⋯ Pair ⋯

*If you want recommendations for the mild in
the custard then check out the previous recipe
on page 75. The below 'Cook' beers are
recommendations for what to use in the crumble.*

Elgood's Apple & Vanilla – UK	Hook Norton Double Stout – UK
Saranac Pumpkin Ale – USA	Napoleone Breakneck Porter – Australia
Floris Apple – Belgium	Antares Porter – Argentina
Iwate Kura Pumpkin – Japan	Basque Oak Brewery Black Gold – Spain
Brooklyn Brewery Post Road Pumpkin Ale – USA	Anderson Valley Barney Flats Oatmeal Stout – USA

Simple NEIPA Mango Sorbet
Makes 1 litre (34 fl oz/4 cups)

Ingredients

2 large, very ripe mangoes, skinned and destoned

120 ml (4 fl oz/½ cup) water

125 g (4 oz/⅔ cup) caster (superfine) sugar (preferably unrefined)

juice of 1 lime

pinch of salt

120 ml (4 fl oz/½ cup) New England IPA

The fashion for New England IPAs, or NEIPAs, may be a very divisive one but there's no doubt the style is here to stay and, when done well, they can be very tasty indeed. With low bitterness and high fruit flavours, they lend themselves very well to this sort of sorbet.

Method

Pop all the ingredients except the beer into a blender and blitz. Stir in the beer and, if you want super-smooth results, pass through a fine sieve or, if you're ok with a few lumps, don't bother.

Spoon into an ice-cream maker and churn until you have a sorbet.

Alternatively, spoon into a tub and freeze, taking it out every half hour or so to rake the sorbet through with a fork until it's frozen.

....

NOTE: New England IPAs are the sexy new kids on the block. Hazy, with negligible bitterness and bursting with huge hop character they are currently dividing the industry whilst bringing more drinkers into the fold.

The problem is, the very nature of them needing so many hops means that very few breweries actually have the means or the skill to make the same beer month in, month out, so I've chosen not to give you brands here, just advice.

You are looking for super-fruity smelling ones, you want to be overwhelmed with waves of mango, lychee, pineapple, apricot and all sorts of other stone fruits.

It's ok to have a hint of turps/diesel/pine but any more than a hint and you want to shy away from them for this recipe, as it won't work.

If it's your thing though, go ahead and enjoy it but it's not mine.

....

Imperiously Nuts Ice Cream
Serves 4

Ingredients

300 g (10½ oz) Jersey milk

290 ml (10 fl oz/generous 1 cup) extra thick double (heavy) cream

1 teaspoon vanilla bean paste

4 large eggs

85 g (3 oz/½ cup) golden caster (superfine) sugar

50 ml (1¾ oz/scant ¼ cup) amaretto

5 Amaretti biscuits, wrapped in a clean tea towel and bashed into small pieces

For the chocolate and imperial stout swirl:

330 g (11 oz) peanut stout/imperial stout

100 g (3½ oz) dark chocolate with 85% cocoa solids

½ gelatine leaf

Cook & Pair

You can use any of these to either make this dish, pair to it, or both!

Tailgate Brewing Peanut Butter Milk Stout – USA

Birrificio del Ducato Verdi – Italy

De Struise Black Albert – Belgium

Cigar City Marshal Zhukov's Imperial Stout – USA

Beavertown Heavy Water – UK

Brasserie du Quercorb Montsegur – France

3 Floyds Dark Lord – USA

Fuller's Imperial Stout – UK

If I do have a dessert when I'm out, it's nearly always ice cream. This indulgent beast is pretty simple to make. I've also promised the other half that I'll make a mint choc chip version one of these days using crème de menthe, which he has an inexplicable fondness for from his college days. So perhaps you could give that a go too if, for some strange reason, you have a bottle kicking around – let me know how it worked.

Method

Mix together the milk and cream in a saucepan, then add the vanilla paste and warm gently.

Meanwhile, cream together the eggs and sugar in a bowl, until the mixture goes pale.

When bubbles start to form around the edge of the milk and cream, take a ladleful and add it to the eggs, whisking vigorously to prevent curdling. Don't stop whisking until it's all incorporated.

Tip the egg mixture back into the saucepan, stir until it's all incorporated and then add the amaretto. Keep heating and stirring slowly for at least 5 minutes until it starts to thicken. A little patience may be required for this – it's done when you can leave a trail through the mixture on the back of the spoon/spatula with your finger.

Cool slightly, then put in the fridge for at least 3 hours. Once it's cooled, sprinkle in the bashed up Amaretti biscuits.

Spoon it in your ice-cream maker and churn. Alternatively, put it in a tub in the freezer and stir round with a fork every 30 minutes or so to break up the ice crystals.

Once the mix is churning, put the stout into a pan and simmer gently to reduce by half. This takes about 20 minutes on a very low heat and you need to be patient or it'll burn and be bitter.

When the stout is nearly reduced, put a heatproof bowl over a saucepan of simmering water, break up the chocolate into the bowl and leave to melt. Soak the gelatine in a little cold water.

By this time the ice cream should be ready. Put into a tub and then place in the freezer.

When the chocolate is melted, whisk it into the stout and, when it's fully amalgamated, whisk in the gelatine squeezed of excess water. Put in the fridge for about 10 minutes to cool slightly so it thickens but doesn't set.

Take the ice cream out of the freezer and make some channels on the surface. Pour the chocolate stout mixture into the channels and then put back in the freezer for 10 minutes or until ready to serve.

Beer
Sausages

You'll need a meat grinder and sausage stuffer for this. You can pick up hand-driven ones at a reasonable price online, or there are also lots of food processor attachments you can buy for various brands, too, which is what I've got for my Kitchen Aid. But do be very specific with your internet search for these things, won't you?

Beer Sausages

Makes about 2.5 kg (5 lb 10 oz) sausages

Ingredients

3 metres (10 ft) natural sausage casings

2.25 kg (5 lb 8 oz) boneless fatty pork shoulder meat, cut into 3 cm (1¼ in) dice

300 ml (10 fl oz/1¼ cups) English-style barley wine

2 teaspoons dried thyme

2½ tablespoons fine sea salt

1½ tablespoons freshly ground black pepper

2 tablespoons panko breadcrumbs (this is optional, if you remove, reduce your liquid by 100 ml/3½ fl oz/scant ½ cup)

....

SPECIALIST EQUIPMENT:

meat grinder

sausage stuffer

....

NOTE: For the beer sausage variations, see page 134. This is the basic method which applies to all of the variations.

....

Making sausages is fun, occasionally frustrating, but ultimately very satisfying and, in my experience, easier as a two-person job.

In his very helpful book, *Charcuterie*, Michael Ruhlman explains the basics so very well and offers insightful tips throughout. Whilst I initially tried just replacing his suggestion of red wine in the basic sausage recipe with beer, I found the level of garlic a little unpalatable (not something I say very often) so, after a few experiments, I hit on the right beer/herb/spice combination that worked for me, and I suggest that's what you do too, because what I like might not be what you like.

And, before you commit to making any of these sausages, make sure you fry off a little of the stuffing to ensure that the seasoning and flavour balance is what you were after or it's a lot of work to be disappointed in!

Finally, unless you have a big family, you might want to consider portioning up the ground, seasoned meat into three servings (reducing your seasonings accordingly) and making three of the different recipes – because three metres of sausages is an awful lot to have of one flavour and the same old sausage all the time can get a little repetitive – but they do freeze perfectly well.

Method

Soak the sausage casings in plenty of cold water overnight.

Put the augur, blades and fine mincing sections of your grinder into the freezer for an hour before grinding the meat.

Put the pork shoulder in a metal bowl and put it the freezer for 20 minutes before you grind the meat.

At the same time, mix together your beer and thyme, in a suitably sized jug.

Take another metal bowl and put it underneath where your grind will drop out. Put 100 ml (3½ fl oz/scant ½ cup) of the beer in the bottom.

Season the pork with the salt and pepper, then start grinding. When you're one-third of the way through, add a third of your beer and thyme mixture. Repeat the process with the beer and thyme mixture until the meat is all ground.

Fold and press the mix together, along with the breadcrumbs, if using, with a rubber spatula until the liquid is absorbed. Then fry a small patty in a pan to check for seasoning. Adjust if necessary, then put the mixture in the fridge for half an hour (you can leave it in the fridge for up to 24 hours at this stage).

When you're ready to make the sausages, prepare the sausage stuffer (trying not to giggle like teenager at the words 'sausage stuffer') and rinse your soaked casings well. Push the casings onto the end of spout of the sausage stuffer and tie off securely at the end, putting a small pin prick in the end, just by the knot.

Take your sausage mix out of the fridge and form into long cylinders, just a bit smaller than the hopper, and feed into the sausage stuffer. If you manage to make them into links, you're a smarter person than I!

Variations

All these variations start life with the same amount of pork, salt and pepper on the basic recipe on page 133 to enable you to make a few different types of sausage from the same base – and all of them follow the same method.

Rauch Chorizo-style Sausages

pork, salt and pepper (see page 133 for measurements)
1 tablespoon smoked paprika
2 tablespoons sweet paprika
1 tablespoon dried oregano
100 ml (3½ fl oz/scant ½ cup) rauchbier (I used Marzen)

Smoked Porter Toulouse

pork, salt and pepper (see page 133 for measurements)
10 garlic cloves (or 3½ tablespoons pre-chopped frozen),
very finely chopped and fried off in a pan with a little oil
for 2 minutes, then allowed to cool
1 tablespoon freshly ground black pepper
(in addition to the base recipe)
½ nutmeg, freshly grated
50 ml (1¾ fl oz/scant ¼ cup) smoked porter

Mildly English with Black Pudding

pork, salt and pepper (see page 133 for measurements)
300 g (10½ oz) black pudding diced into 2 cm (¾ in) cubes
2 onions, blitzed to a paste in a food processor
12 sage leaves, picked and blitzed with the onion
¼ nutmeg, freshly grated
50 ml (1½ fl oz/3 tablespoons) English-style dark mild

Beer Mustard

Makes four 250 g (9 oz) jars

Ingredients

175 g (6 oz) yellow mustard seeds

175 g (6 oz) black mustard seeds

175 ml (6 fl oz/¾ cup) cider or Beer Vinegar (page 141)

1 teaspoon English mustard powder

300 ml (10 fl oz/1¼ cups) local beer, not too bitter

2 teaspoons fine sea salt

4 tablespoons heather honey

This is simplicity itself. Use a beer local to you that isn't too bitter. As my closest brewery is Kew Brewery, I use the Botanic, which has a hint of juniper in it (see also Beer-brined Corned Beef on page 156 for juniper ale use).

Method

Soak the mustard seeds in the beer overnight at room temperature.

When you're ready to make the mustard, sterilise your jars and the lids in a large pot of boiling water.

Reserve 2 tablespoons of the grains of the mustard seeds and then put all the other ingredients in a food processor and blitz until smooth. Stir through the reserved mustard seeds and spoon into the sterilised jars.

You can use it immediately but it's better if left for a week before using as it mellows and amalgamates better.

Recipe photo overleaf

Compound
Butters

Compound butters are an awesome weapon to have in your food arsenal. They can enliven a meal at the drop of a hat and make you seem like a kitchen deity when people express surprise and delight at the simple meal you've elevated to restaurant level without breaking a sweat. These are the three that I find the most useful to give things a little kick but, honestly, play around with your own ideas – it's not expensive and takes up very little space in your fridge for fantastic returns.

Compound Butters

Each makes about 100 g (3½ oz)

NOTE: This is the basic method which applies to all of the variations.

Method

Take one 250 g (9 oz) pat of unsalted butter and divide it roughly into three parts, then allow to soften in separate bowls. Add the 3 different flavourings below to each bowl, incorporate well into the butter, then form into a cylinder by rolling in cling film (plastic wrap) and store in the fridge until needed.

Obviously, if you hit on one that really works for you, then scale up the ingredients by three to use a whole pat of butter.

Flanders Oud Bruin with Dates & Cumin

Ingredients
2 dates, stoned
100 ml (3½ fl oz/scant ½ cup) Flanders Oud Bruin-style (Flanders red will also work here if you can't source Oud Bruin)
½ teaspoon fine sea salt
1 teaspoon ground cumin

Method
Soak the dates in the beer for 1 hour.
Take the dates out and blitz in a blender with 2 tablespoons of the beer, the salt and cumin. Then follow the method above.

Smoked Paprika & Apricot Wheat
(or Belgian-style will do but apricot is nicer)

Ingredients
2 teaspoons smoked paprika
2 teaspoons apricot wheat beer
½ teaspoon fine sea salt

Method
Blend all the ingredients together into a paste. Then follow the method above.

American Red with Wakame & Miso

Ingredients
1 teaspoon dried wakame seaweed
½ teaspoon coarse sea salt
1 tablespoon red miso paste
1 tablespoon American red ale

Method
Combine the wakame and salt, then blend into the miso paste and finally mix in the beer. Then follow the method above.

SOME EFFORT

Beer Chutney

Makes about four 500 g (1 lb 2 oz) jars

Ingredients

1 kg (2 lb 4 oz) ripe plums, stoned and quartered if small, cut into eighths if large

500 g (1 lb 2 oz) cooking apples, peeled, cored and finely cubed

500 g (1 lb 2 oz) white or yellow onion, finely chopped

100 g (3½ oz/¾ cup) sultanas (golden raisins)

100 g (3½ oz/¾ cup) dried sour cherries

1 Scotch bonnet chilli, chopped

2 tablespoons dill or fennel seeds

2 tablespoons yellow mustard seeds

1 teaspoon English mustard powder

300 g (10½ oz/1½ cups) granulated sugar

200 g (7 oz/1 cup) demerara sugar

300 ml (10 fl oz/1¼ cups) blood orange beer

200 ml (7 fl oz/scant 1 cup) Beer Vinegar (see opposite) or cider vinegar

This is another one of those really flexible recipes that you can easily personalise depending on what is available.

This particular recipe came from a quick half hour scrumping little tiny super-sweet plums with the biggest naughty kid I know – my Dad. Scrumping, for those of you not familiar with the term, is 'collecting' fruit that's 'going to waste', although there's a strong chance that it's not always on public land … I believe the posh term for it these days is foraging. Although, come to think of it, I've never seen a forager run away from a very angry old man because me and my sister were stealing, oh, no, hang on, 'scrumping', his cobnuts for our granddad. However, I've become distracted with tales of my misspent youth, here's what I did with my ill-gotten gains from my day out with my Dad.

Method

Put all the ingredients into a saucepan and simmer gently until you can trace a trail in the back of a spoon. This will take 50–60 minutes.

Whilst that's bubbling gently, wash your jars with hot soapy water, rinse them well and put in a low oven (don't put any rubber seals in the oven, just pop those in some boiling water just before you're going to use them and fish out with some tongs).

When your chutney is sufficiently reduced, pop it in the jars, seal with lids, and put in a cool, dark place to develop for at least 3 months.

Cook

Blood orange beers aren't always the easiest to get hold of, bit like the fruits themselves really, but lots of breweries do seasonal ones, the ones listed on the right are pretty regularly produced but keep your ear to the ground for ones that are released sporadically as well. Alternatively, you could use other citrus beers.

21st Amendment Brew Free or Die Blood Orange – USA

Adnams Blood Orange Wheat – UK

Flying Dog Bloodline Ale – USA

Dogfish head Flesh & Blood IPA – USA

Jack's Abby Blood Orange Wheat – USA

Recipe photo on page 138

Beer Vinegar

Makes as much as you want

Ingredients

beer of choice (just a hint: really highly hopped beers often kill the vinegar mother, so DIPA is probably out)

for every 500 ml (17 fl oz/2 cups) of beer you need ½ teaspoon of liquid sugar, such as corn syrup, maple syrup or glucose

1 bottle of unpasteurised vinegar with an obvious mother in it (kind of a floating ectoplasm)

squares of muslin (cheesecloth)

small elastic bands or string

I hesitate to call this a recipe, really – it's more of a shopping list and a few instructions… which I suppose, on reflection, is the essence of a recipe. Metaphysical conundrums aside, I just don't think people know how easy it is to make your own vinegar and it can be made with beers that might otherwise go down the drain or be drunk grudgingly.

My personal favourite beer to make vinegar with is a Belgian-style quadrupel. It comes out somewhere between a sherry and a malt vinegar and is very sophisticated but still has a bit of an acetic wallop. However, experiment to your heart's content. Want a lighter style of vinegar? Go for a blonde ale. Want a heavy dark one? Use an imperial stout. It's not rocket science but the results can be sensational.

Method

When you're getting down to the bottom of your vinegar bottle with the mother in, now is the time to plan your beer vinegar.

Prepare enough sterilised bottles to contain the amount of vinegar you want to make.

Put the beer in a mixing bowl and for every 500 ml (17 fl oz/2 cups), add ½ teaspoon of liquid sugar.

Mix until dissolved. Add the end of the vinegar, making sure you get the mother in there, and stir vigorously.

Put the vinegar in the sterilised jars and secure the muslin around the necks. Put somewhere warm and dark for 2–3 months.

When the vinegar is ready, remove the muslin and screw on the caps.

....

NOTE: Make sure you store the bottle caps somewhere safe, as you'll be needing them when the vinegar is ready!

....

Recipe photo on page 138

SHOW OFF

We all like a little show off every now and then.
A lot of these recipes are the showstoppers you're
looking for on that front so, go on, make them
and take in the praise – you're worth it.

Sour Beer Scallop Ceviche
Serves 4

Ingredients

8 large, plump scallops

300 ml (10 fl oz/1¼ cups) Berliner Weisse (passionfruit or citrus for preference)

½ teaspoon fine sea salt

¼ teaspoon very, very finely chopped red chilli

micro herb radish or salad cress, to garnish

Ceviche is simplicity itself but it takes some knowledge and care about what it is you're doing to make it a success. The first thing is to make sure you get your scallops from a reputable source and that they're incredibly fresh. Fresh scallops should be firm, opalescent and can come with or without roe. If yours have roe, then don't waste it, it's delicious.

Reserve it and fry it incredibly quickly in butter and place in the middle of your circle of ceviche for an added touch of luxury.

Method

Remove any muscle from the side of the scallop and place in the freezer for 15 minutes.

Mix together the beer and salt until the salt is dissolved, keep cold.

Slice each scallop as thinly as you can and lay in a single layer in a shallow, non-metallic dish. Pour over the beer mix.

Leave for 3–5 minutes, or until the scallops start to turn opaque.

Gently lift the scallops out of the beer, portion the slices out evenly and arrange in a circle on small plates, sprinkle the chilli evenly across all the plates and garnish with your cress or micro herbs.

Cook & Pair

You can use any of these for either the cooking or the pairing aspect – enjoy!

Westbrook Gose – USA

Magic Rock Salty Kiss – UK

10 Barrel Cucumber Crush – USA

Berliner Kindl – Germany

Wayward Brewing Sourpuss – Australia

8 Wired Brewing Cucumber Hippy – New Zealand

Original Ritterguts Gose – Germany

Mikkeller Drink'In Berliner – Denmark

Dugges Tropic Thunder – Sweden

Cervejaria Narcose Flip Flops to Heaven – Brazil

Wheat-beer Poached Crayfish Tails with Lime Pickle Yoghurt

Serves 4

Ingredients

For the crayfish:

16 crayfish (you can substitute tiger prawns (shrimps) if you can't get crayfish)

300 ml (10 fl oz/1¼ cups) Belgian wheat beer

½ teaspoon fine sea salt

zest of ½ orange

For the radishes:

15 g (½ oz/1 tablespoon) fine sea salt

8 g (¼ oz/1½ teaspoons) caster (superfine) sugar

20 ml (¾ fl oz/generous 1 tablespoon) hot water

330 ml (11¼ fl oz/1⅓ cups) well-chilled plain Berliner weisse

50 ml (1¾ fl oz/scant ¼ cup) white wine vinegar

8 large pink radishes, sliced on the finest setting of the mandoline

cold water, if needed, to top up

For the lime pickle yoghurt:

2 tablespoons shop-bought lime pickle

4 tablespoons goat's milk yoghurt (or thick natural yoghurt)

¼ teaspoon radish pickling liquid

For the garnish:

½ sharp green eating (dessert) apple, like Granny Smith, cut into matchsticks

juice of ½ orange

micro radish

As any fan of Indian food will know, the pickles and chutneys that come from the Indian sub-continent are a thing of beauty, and I'm a huge fan of lime pickle in particular. However, it's often a bit on the searingly hot side, even for me, so this idea came to me when I was piling equal amounts of lime pickle and yoghurt onto a poppadum one evening (I know, I'm all class).

You can make this as an amuse bouche or as a light starter. If you want it as a starter then double the ingredients, but I really like this as a small palate livener before the main event, it can be made a few hours in advance but take it out of the fridge 15 minutes before you need it.

Method

To cook the crayfish, put them in a saucepan with the beer, salt and orange zest and gently bring to a low simmer. Cook for 3 minutes, then turn off the heat and allow to rest in the pan for another 5 minutes.

Lift the crayfish out and remove the tail meat (freeze the shells for making bisque on page 160). Place on a plate lined with paper towel in the fridge.

Prepare the radishes. Put the salt and sugar in a large, non-metallic bowl, and add the hot water. Stir vigorously to dissolve.

Add the beer and white wine vinegar, then the radishes. Add enough cold water, if needed, to cover the radishes, then refrigerate for no longer than 2 hours before using.

To make the lime pickle yoghurt, put all the ingredients into a blender, blitz until smooth, then refrigerate.

Prepare the garnish by tossing the apple in the orange juice to stop it going brown, then refrigerate.

Using either squat glass tumblers or a small plate, arrange a circle of the pickled radishes. Top with 4 of the crayfish tails, slim end of the tail pointing inwards. Drizzle the tails with the lime pickle yoghurt and garnish with apple and micro radish.

Cook

Rivière d'Ain Thou — France

Camden Gentleman's Wit — UK

Wäls Witte — Brazil

Feral White — Australia

Pair

Avery White Rascal — USA

Brasserie Lefebvre Blanche de Bruxelles — Belgium

Williams Bros Grozet — UK

Hitachino Nest White Ale — Japan

Full
English

Breakfast in a pie – the dream, right? Right.

Individual Full English Breakfast Pies with Bean Gravy & Gooey Eggs

Serves 6

Ingredients

For the shortcrust pastry:

500 g (1 lb 2 oz/4 cups) plain (all-purpose) flour, plus extra for dusting

¼ teaspoon icing (confectioners') sugar

¼ teaspoon sea salt

125 g (4 oz) well-chilled unsalted butter, cubed, plus extra for greasing

125 g (4 oz) well-chilled lard, cubed

3–5 tablespoons well-chilled rauchbier/smoked porter or stout (reserve the rest for the filling)

For the filling:

150 g (5 oz) dried wild mushrooms, soaked in warm water

24 cocktail sausages (or 8 ordinary chipolatas, twisted and cut into 3 small sausages each)

200 g (7 oz) black pudding, cut into 2 cm (¾ in) cubes

175 g (6 oz) good-quality smoked bacon lardons (pieces)

400 g (14 oz) tin of baked beans

2 tablespoons Worcestershire sauce

2 tablespoons tomato ketchup

1 tablespoon brown sauce (I use Tiptree for preference, but HP is fine)

2 teaspoons chilli sauce (I use Cholula but Tabasco is fine)

200 ml (7 fl oz/scant 1 cup) rauchbier

fine sea salt (optional)

For the eggs:

14 quail's eggs, at room temperature (I've made provision for 2 breaking during the peeling process!)

a bowl of iced water

For the egg wash:

1 medium egg

1 tablespoon Worcestershire sauce

At the risk of sounding as old as the hills, when I joined the pub trade paper at the age of 23 as a junior reporter it was still a very analogue place. I had to fight tooth and nail to get email in the office and even then, I regret to report, you would access the internet through dial up, a screeching noise that will never leave anyone who heard it.

That meant face-to-face relationships were vital and I'll never forget my first 'rentaquote' licensee, Carl Smith who, in tandem with his wife Pauline, ran two iconic Mayfair pubs called the Guinea and the Windmill – the latter being so famous for its pies that Carl was asked to stop entering the National Pie Championships by the organisers because his steak and kidney kept wiping the floor with the competition. One of Carl's madder inventions was the breakfast pie and this is my homage to that.

....

NOTE: Don't be intimidated by the length of this recipe; it's just lots of small, simple steps that make up a rather glorious whole! You need to start with the eggs at least the day before. You can prep all the other elements ahead of time to make it simplicity itself to prepare if you're feeling a bit 'delicate' on the day.

You'll need a 6-hole muffin/Yorkshire pudding tin (pan) with 9 cm wide x 6 cm deep (3½ in x 2½ in) holes.

....

Cook

I can't, in all good conscience, suggest you drink with breakfast, so I'm afraid if you want to do that then you'll have to make your own decisions!

Alaskan Smoked Porter – USA

To Øl Smoke on the Porter – Denmark

Okell's Aile – UK

Aecht Schlenkerla Märzen – Germany

Ölvishot Brugghús Lava – Iceland

To make the pastry, sift the flour, icing sugar and salt into a large mixing bowl. Rub the butter and lard into the flour until the mixture resembles breadcrumbs.

Add just 2 tablespoons of the cold beer and, using a rubber spatula, bring together into a 'shaggy' dough.

Using the same spatula, fold the mixture into the dough – don't stir. Add more liquid if needed.

When it comes together in a craggy ball, wrap in cling film (plastic wrap) and chill in the refrigerator overnight.

To prepare the filling, soak the mushrooms in a little warm water for a few minutes. Drain but reserve the liquid, and set aside.

Put a large frying pan (skillet) on a medium-low heat and brown the sausages, black pudding and bacon gently until cooked and lightly browned. Drain on paper towels, then leave to cool and put in the refrigerator.

In a food processor, add the beans, Worcestershire sauce, ketchup, brown sauce and chilli sauce. Start to blitz, adding as much beer as it takes to loosen the mixture slightly to the consistency of a thick gravy (around 4–6 tablespoons). Season with salt, if required. Reserve any remaining beer in a pot in the fridge along with the baked bean 'gravy'.

To cook the eggs, fill a medium saucepan two-thirds full with well-salted water and bring to a gentle simmer over a medium heat. Put the bowl of iced water next to the hob and set a timer for 2 minutes 15 seconds.

Using a fine, shallow sieve, gently add the quail's eggs to the hot water and simmer for exactly 2 minutes 15 seconds. Scoop out and place straight in the bowl of iced water, stirring them very gently for a few minutes.

Prepare a large enough plastic container with a layer of oiled cling film, to place the cooked quail's eggs in a single layer.

One by one, take the quail's eggs out of the iced water and, with gentle firmness, tap the pointed end of the egg on a solid surface. Repeat with the rounder end, then gently peel the shell away. Be careful – the egg is very soft. Place carefully in the container and repeat until all the eggs are done. Put them in the freezer.

On the day of eating, remove the cooked meats, bean 'gravy', mushrooms and pastry from the fridge. Preheat the oven to 180°C (350°F/Gas 4) and put a baking tray (sheet) on a rack in the middle of the oven. Lightly grease the muffin tin (pan).

Cut the pastry into 3 pieces and set one-third aside for the lids. Reform the other 2 pieces and cut into 6. Roll out each piece on a lightly floured surface and cut into a circle roughly twice as large as the muffin tin holes are round. Use to line the muffin tin.

Line the pastry with scrumpled baking parchment, equally divide baking beans between them, place on the baking tray and blind bake for 10 minutes (don't worry about any overhang, these are supposed to look rustic).

Remove the beans and paper and return to the oven for a further 3 minutes. Allow to cool slightly.

Cut the reserved pastry into 6 pieces and roll out to half the thickness of the pastry base to form the lids.

To make an egg wash, mix the egg with the Worcestershire sauce. Put your baking tray back in the oven.

To assemble your pies, put a layer of the soaked mushrooms in the bottom of each pie, then a layer of bacon, then 2 sausages, then black pudding, then 2 more sausages. Finally, when all the pies are filled, get the quail's eggs out of the freezer and gently put them on the top.

Equally divide the baked bean gravy between the pies (just enough to come up to below the eggs as it will expand and bubble up as it heats). You won't use it all.

Run a little egg wash around the edge of the baked pastry and top with the lid. Press down gently with a fork to provide a small crimp and cut a small hole in the top to allow the steam to escape. Egg wash the pies well and gently put them on the pre-heated baking tray. Bake for 8 minutes.

By that time you should see steam coming out of the tops. Egg wash again, turn the oven off but leave the door tightly closed for another 5 minutes.

Transfer the pies to a wire rack to cool for 5 minutes in the tin.

Meanwhile, add the remainder of the beer and a few tablespoons of the reserved mushroom liquid to the baked bean gravy and warm in a pan. Pour into a heatproof jug.

Use a flexible pallette knife to free the pastry from the sides of the muffin tins and then gently ease them out. Cut into the pies quickly and serve with the gravy.

You should find that the yolks on the eggs are still just very slightly runny or at least fudgy.

Pumpkin Season
Serves 2

Ingredients

2 soup-bowl-sized edible squashes as equally sized as you can find

a pinch of fine sea salt

a pinch of smoked sea salt (optional)

80 g (3 oz) cauliflower, grated or pulsed in the food processor to look like breadcrumbs

225 ml (8 fl oz/scant 1 cup) double (heavy) cream

150 ml (5 fl oz/scant ⅔ cup) Farmhouse ale

1 bouquet garni made up of: 6 sage leaves, 2 bay leaves, 4 squished garlic cloves, 4 sprigs of thyme, 2 sprigs of rosemary, tied together

200 g (7 oz) macaroni or chifferi rigati

1 tablespoons cornflour (cornstarch)

knob of butter

splash of basic olive oil

10 grinds of freshly ground black pepper

150 g (5 oz) good-quality mature Cheddar, grated

175 g (6 oz) Gouda or Emmental (Swiss cheese), finely chopped

40 g (1½ oz) Stinking Bishop or Tallegio, finely chopped

100 g (3½ oz) chorizo picante, finely diced and fried until crispy (optional)

chilli (hot pepper) flakes (optional)

20 g (¾ oz) Parmesan, grated

A bowl that you can eat has to be the ultimate in greedy delight, and these pumpkins look so pretty when baked and bubbling with cheesey, cauliflowery pasta goodness, they're almost irresistible. If you'd like to make this vegetarian then substitute your cheeses appropriately and omit the chorizo. Replace it with the pumpkin seeds you've scooped out, toasted in a dry pan until golden and tossed in smoked paprika instead.

Cook & Pair

You can interchange any of the beers from cooking to pairing here.

North End Botanicole – New Zealand

Burning Sky Saison à la Provision – UK

La Sirene Saison – Australia

Saison Dupont – Belgium

Boulevard Brewing Saison Brett – US

Two Brothers Domaine DuPage – US

St Armand French Country Ale – France

Brewery Ommegang Hennepin – USA

St Feuillien Saison – Belgium

Crooked Stave Surette – USA

Recipe method overleaf

Method

Preheat the oven to 170°C (340°F/Gas 3) and heat a baking tray (sheet).

Cut the top 5 cm (2 in), horizontally, off the squashes, set this 'lid' aside, scoop out the innards (reserving the seeds), season the inside of the squash lightly with fine salt (smoked if you want to use it) and pepper. Repeat with the inside of the 'lids'.

If needed, take a very thin slice off the bottom of the squash to ensure it sits stably.

Take an arms' length of kitchen foil and fold it lengthways three times to create a long, thin 'belt'. Wrap around the squashes and gently tie to help prevent splitting.

Put the lids back on the squashes, leaving a small gap to allow steam inside to escape, place on the heated baking tray in the oven for 30 minutes to soften and cook.

Meanwhile, put the cauliflower, cream and ale in a saucepan with the bouquet garni over a low heat. Don't allow to boil.

Put a saucepan of well-salted water on to boil. Add the pasta, stirring after a few minutes. After 5 minutes, take 2 tablespoons of the starchy water and mix it with the cornflour to make a paste.

After 7 minutes, the pasta should be quite al dente, so drain, (reserving some more of the pasta water in case you need it for the sauce), then put back in the pan and mix with the knob of butter and a tiny splash of olive oil to stop it sticking together. Toss so it distributes equally.

Take the bouquet garni out of the cream mixture, add the cornflour and the black pepper. Mix in all but a few handfuls of the different cheeses with the cream.

Using a hand-held blender, blitz the sauce. It should start to thicken quite quickly but if it gets too thick, just add a bit more pasta water. Check for seasoning and adjust accordingly.

Mix the cheese sauce and pasta and spoon into the squashes, pop the lids back on, turn the oven down to 150°C (300°F/Gas 1) and cook for 20 minutes. Take the lids off, top with the reserved cheese, sprinkle with chorizo and chilli flakes, if using, and grated Parmesan. Remove the foil 'belts' and turn the oven up to 170°C (340°F/Gas 3) and bake for another 10–15 minutes until golden and bubbly.

Leave to rest for 8–10 minutes before serving.

Beer-brined Corned Beef

Yields about 2.5 kg (5 lb 10 oz) corned beef (easily halved, just reduce cooking the time to about 6 hours)

·········· Ingredients ··········

4 litres (140 fl oz/17 cups) water

450 g (1 lb) sea salt

50 g (2 oz) smoked sea salt

25 g (1 oz) pink curing salt (optional)

4 garlic cloves, smashed

1.2 litres (40 fl oz/4¾ cups) juniper ale, chilled

2.5 kg (5 lb 10 oz) beef brisket

500 ml (17 fl oz/2 cups) gresette, farmhouse or gruit ale

25 ml (1½ tablespoons) bourbon

500 ml (17 fl oz/2 cups) mushroom stock (optional)

For the pickling spice mix:

20 g (¾ oz) black mustard seeds

25 g (1 oz) coriander seeds

2 teaspoons allspice berries

2 teaspoons voatsiperifery peppercorns

2 teaspoons lampung black peppercorns

1 teaspoon white peppercorns

2 teaspoons chilli (hot pepper) flakes

2 cascabel chillies, deseeded and chopped

8 g (¼ oz) blade mace

1 small cinnamon stick

½ teaspoon whole cloves

1 teaspoon fennel seeds

1 teaspoon celery seed

2 teaspoons dill seed

generous 1 teaspoon ground ginger

20 dried bay leaves, crumbled

½ teaspoon dried wakame seaweed

That moment when you first taste proper corned beef is a revelatory one. For me it was only about 10 years ago, before that my experiences were with the dubious, mystery meat, tinned variety that comes in a tin that seems designed solely to slice your thumb off! Just a quick bit of advice, the pickling spice is also delicious for pickling vegetables.

···········

NOTE: You should be able to source voatsiperifery and lampung peppercorns online.

···········

······ Cook ······· Pair ······

Ultimately the pairings for this will depend on what it is you do with it. However, you can't really go wrong with any of the following.

Cook	Pair
Williams Bros. Fraoch – UK	Tripel Karmeliet – Belgium
Jopen Koyt – Netherlands	Unibroue La Fin du Monde – Canada
Troll Febre Alta – Italy	Westmalle Tripel – Belgium
La Choulettee Biere de Sans Cullottes – France	Wäls Trippel – Brazil
Little Earth Project Hedgerow – UK	St Austell Bad Habit – UK

Method

Start by making the pickling spice mix. Simply dry-fry all the whole spices, adding the bigger more robust ones like allspice first and the more delicate ones like dill seed later (don't fry the ground ginger, bay leaves or seaweed).

To brine the meat, put the water in a saucepan over a medium heat, add the salts and stir until dissolved. Remove from the heat and add 3 tablespoons of the pickling spice and garlic, then add the chilled ale, which will help bring the temperature down more quickly.

Pour the brine into a non-metallic tub or sealable bag (ziplock or vacuum is fine), then add the brisket and refrigerate for 5–7 days; no longer or it gets too salty.

To cook the meat, wash brisket clean of pickling spices, place in a large, ovenproof pan with a lid filled with cold water and bring to the boil. Drain and discard water.

Pour the chosen beer and bourbon into the pan. In a muslin bag, add 5 tablespoons of the pickling spice and place in the pan with the mushroom stock, if using, then top up with enough water to just cover the meat. Place the lid on top and cook in your oven at 90°C (194°F/Gas ¼), for 2½–3½ hours, topping up with more water if required. The meat should have a lovely open texture and be really tender (do try and use an oven thermometer, you'll get better results).

Allow to cool in the cooking liquor before handling. Don't discard the liquor; it can make a tasty sauce base (see tip).

TIP: My favourite way to serve this is sliced in a bread roll with some sauerkraut and yoghurt. Simpley deglaze the pan with some of the reserved cooking liquor and return meat to the pan for a few moments. Put in a bread roll filled with sauerkraut tossed in yoghurt and some grain mustard.

SHOW OFF

Turbot with a Creamy Beer, Samphire & Cockle Broth
Serves 4

Ingredients

1 medium-sized turbot, filleted into 4 fillets

400 g (14 oz) new potatoes

150 ml (5 fl oz/scant ⅔ cup) Belgian wheat beer

150 ml (5 fl oz/scant ⅔ cup) double (heavy) cream

pared peel and juice from ½ unwaxed lemon (reserve other half to dress dish at end)

pared peel and juice from 1 clementine

2 tablespoons basic olive oil

2 tablespoons plain (all-purpose) flour

2 teaspoons salt

knob of unsalted butter

300 g (10½ oz) pre-prepared cockles, well rinsed (option to reserve 100 g/3½ oz for the cockle popcorn, see below)

100 g (3½ oz) samphire

25 g (1 oz) finely chopped chives (or 10 g (½ oz) of wild garlic if in season)

salt and freshly ground black pepper

For the cockle popcorn (optional):

2 tablespoons cornflour (cornstarch)

2 tablespoons coriander seeds, dry-fried and finely ground

1 tablespoon Sichuan peppercorns, dry-fried and finely ground

100 g (3½ oz) pre-prepared cockles, reserved from main recipe

groundnut, grapeseed or other neutral oil, for deep-frying or shallow-frying

pinch of fine sea salt

You will almost certainly need to go to a fishmonger for turbot. It is expensive so you could always replace it with monkfish, john dory or even sustainably caught cod or haddock. This dish will work equally well with a smaller amount of dill rather than chives or wild garlic if that allium bite isn't your thing.

Method

If you are going to make the popcorn, do it first. Mix together the cornflour and spices in a large bowl.

Drop the cockles into the bowl and toss until well covered. Sift them out from the residual flour.

Heat some oil in a deep-fat fryer or a large heavy-based frying pan (skillet), add the cockles, cover and deep- or shallow-fry them until they stop sizzling. It should only take a few minutes. It is safer to do this in a deep fryer with a cover, if you can, but if not then make sure you've got a flare guard for the frying pan.

Turn out onto paper towels, drain and season with fine sea salt. Reserve in a warm oven until ready to serve (if you can resist eating them!).

To cook the fish, take the fillets out of the fridge and make shallow slashes in the skin.

Put a pan of salted water on to boil for the potatoes and preheat the oven to 140°C (275°F/Gas 1).

Put the beer, cream and citrus pared peels in another pan with a pinch of salt and heat very, very gently – do not allow it to boil.

While the cream and beer broth is reducing gently, cook the new potatoes in the boiling water until soft, then drain, return to the pan, and cut in half when cool enough to handle.

Put the sliced potatoes on a baking tray (sheet) and place in the oven.

Meanwhile, heat a heavy-based frying pan to medium-high heat, then add the oil.

Mix the flour and salt. Dust the turbot fillets with the seasoned flour, then place skin-side down in the hot oil. They should sizzle immediately. Turn the heat down to medium-low and cook for about 4 minutes. When the fish still has a clear line of translucent flesh in the middle, turn the fish over and add the knob of butter to the pan. Turn off the heat and leave to finish cooking in the residual heat.

Remove the peel from the cream mixture and add the cockles and samphire. Add the cooking juices from the fish with the lemon and clementine juice and then finally the chives or wild garlic. Stir.

Take the potatoes out of the oven and dish out onto serving plates. Spoon over the samphire and cockle broth then lay the turbot fillets on top. Finish with the cockle popcorn, a fresh grind of pepper and serve.

Cook ········· ∥ ········· Pair ·····

Rivière d'Ain
Thou – France

Avery White
Rascal – USA

Camden
Gentleman's Wit
– UK

Brasserie Lefebvre
Blanche de
Bruxelles
– Belgium

Wäls Witte
– Brazil

Williams Bros
Grozet – UK

Feral White
– Australia

Hitachino Nest
White Ale – Japan

Gueuze-poached Cod's Roe & Crab Pasta in a Prawn & Fennel Bisque

Serves 4

Ingredients

For the bisque:

225 g (8 oz) raw tiger prawns (shrimp) in their shells

1 teaspoon groundnut, grapeseed or other neutral oil, for frying

130 g (4 oz) fennel (to yield 100 g/3½ oz), chopped (any fronds reserved)

1 large onion, chopped, or 100 g (3½ oz) pre-chopped frozen onions

50 g (2 oz) celery sticks, chopped into 2 cm (¾ in) chunks

50 g (2 oz) carrot, chopped into 2 cm (¾ in) cubes

200 g (7 oz) tinned cherry tomatoes

500 ml (17 fl oz/2 cups) shellfish or fish stock

¼ teaspoon hot sauce

¼ teaspoon paprika

100 ml (3½ fl oz/scant ½ cup) barley wine, can be barrel-aged

75 ml (2½ fl oz/5 tablespoons) double (heavy) cream

fennel fronds, chopped (optional)

For the pasta:

65 g (2¼ oz/heaped ½ cup) semolina flour

65 g (2¼ oz/heaped ½ cup) 00 pasta flour, plus extra for dusting

80 g (3 oz) egg yolk

20 g (¾ oz) egg white

pinch of fine sea salt

For the ravioli filling:

1 unwaxed lemon, grated zest reserved

1 teaspoon fine sea salt

200 ml (7 fl oz/scant 1 cup) gueuze

75 g (2½ oz) cod's roe

150 g (5 oz) picked white crab meat

1½ tablespoons goat's milk yoghurt

4 tablespoons finely chopped chives

4 grinds of freshly ground pepper

extra-virgin olive oil, to finish

salmon caviar, to finish

This dish mainly came about because it seems that people are either scared of cod's roe or don't know what to do with it, outside of the smoked stuff being made into taramasalata – which is nice when well made – but it's a versatile and tasty ingredient that I think needs a bit more love.

Because cod's roe is quite rich, using gueuze to poach it in gives it a lighter edge, a hint of earthy acidity that infuses right through it, making it more approachable. And bisque is something that genuinely terrified me the first time I thought of making it. Having only ever eaten it in fine dining establishments, it has an air of 'elite soup' about it, but it's actually simplicity itself – it just requires a little patience, a strong blender and a fine sieve.

In my opinion, you will need a pasta maker for this. If you don't own one and don't plan on making lots of pasta, I suggest you borrow one from a friend or neighbour – they take up a lot of cupboard space – I have a pasta-making attachment for my Kitchen Aid attachment, which also save a bit of elbow grease.

NOTE: For the gueuze-poached roe, you can use any of the classic Belgian gueuzes but if you can't get hold of one of those, then most farmhouse ales will do the job nicely, see page 152 for details. The beers in the 'Cook/Pair' section of the box refer to the bisque.

Method

Prepare the bisque. Shell the prawns and fry the shells over a medium-high heat in oil for 5 minutes. Add the fennel, onions, celery and carrot and stir. Add the tomatoes, stock, hot sauce and paprika and half of the beer and simmer gently for 30 minutes.

Leave to cool slightly, add the prawns, then blitz with a hand-held blender or in a food processor. Push through a fine sieve into a clean saucepan as hard as possible. Add the cream and stir. Set aside.

To make the pasta, mix the flours in a bowl, and in a separate bowl whisk the eggs together with the salt.

Make a well in the middle of the flour and pour the egg mix in, slowly pulling the flour in, mixing as you go, to bring together into a dough. Knead for 10–15 minutes, then wrap in cling film (plastic wrap) and put in the fridge for 2 hours.

To make the ravioli filling, put half the zested lemon, ½ teaspoon of the salt, gueuze and the cod's roe into a small saucepan and add a little water, if needed, to cover the roe. Bring it to just below a boil and cook, turning occasionally, for 5 minutes. Turn the heat off and leave the roe to cool in the gueuze.

When the roe is cooled, put it in a mixing bowl, peel off and discard the skin and mix with the crab meat, goat's milk yoghurt and ½ teaspoon of the chives, pepper and gently fold together.

Put the mixture in the fridge until required.

Put a large pot of heavily salted water on the hob to boil. Take the pasta dough out of the fridge and cut in half. Heat the oven to just warm and put your pasta bowls in.

Roll out the dough, then, using a pasta roller, run through from the thickest to the thinnest setting, making sure you keep your pasta lightly floured and nice and elastic. Roll out 2 pieces around 30 × 12 cm (12 × 4½ in) long.

Put 12 even dollops of the roe mixture evenly spaced on one of the pasta strips. Brush around the filling with a little water, roll out and lay over your other sheet of pasta and form your raviolis, using the sides of your little fingers to encircle the mixture to ensure you push any air out. Cut them out in even squares or circles.

Put the bisque on to warm over a gentle heat and add the remaining half of the beer. Put a double layer of paper towels on a board.

Slide the ravioli into the boiling water and cook for a few minutes until they all float.

Divide the warmed bisque between 4 bowls and when the pasta is done, gently lift it out, draining it briefly on the paper towels.

Lay 3 ravioli in the middle of the bisque, dot and swirl the bisque with the extra-virgin olive oil and garnish in the middle of the ravioli with the salmon caviar and fennel fronds, if using, remaining chives and lemon zest.

Cook

Cheshire Brewhouse Conger Tun – UK

Cameron's Brewing Where the Buffalo Roam – USA

Sierra Nevada Bigfoot – USA

Adnams Tally-Ho – UK

De Molen Bommen & Granaten – Netherlands

Pair

JW Lees Harvest Ale – UK

Traquair House Jacobite Ale – UK

Batemans Victory Ale – UK

AleSmith Old Numbskull – USA

Pork Pie

Serves 12–14

Ingredients

For the jelly:

bones from meat listed in the filling ingredients (below)

2 pig's trotters, split lengthways

1 large carrot, cut into chunks

1 large celery stick, cut into chunks

1 onion, cut into chunks

1 fresh bay leaf

300 ml (10 fl oz/1¼ cups) Amber beer

4 tablespoons Beer Chutney (page 140), blitzed until smooth

For the filling:

½ teaspoon ground mace

1 allspice berry

2 teaspoons coarse sea salt

3 white peppercorns

½ teaspoon freshly grated nutmeg

1 teaspoon anchovy paste

2 tablespoons English-style bitter

900 g (2 lb) pork shoulder cut into 2 cm (¾ in) dice, bone and skin reserved

400 g (14 oz) ham hock meat, cut into 2 cm (¾ in) dice, bone and skin reserved

300 g (10½ oz) rindless streaky unsmoked bacon, chopped into 2 cm (¾ in) pieces

3 tablespoons thyme leaves, finely chopped (roughly 8 stems, stripped of leaves)

6 sage leaves, finely chopped

There is little that will make you more popular than staggering into a party under the weight of a giant pie (with obvious apologies to the vegans and vegetarians reading this!). I can't stress strongly enough that getting good-quality, high-welfare meat and fresh-bought herbs and spices for this is essential.

You'll need a good butcher for this. Call ahead of time, tell them what you're planning and how much you need and they'll do all the hard work of de-boning and chopping the meat for you – also ask them to do the mincing part if you don't have a mincer.

You need a 20 cm (8 in) non-stick springform cake tin (pan) for this and I highly recommend using a digital thermometer to ensure you don't overcook the pie. There's also enough pastry in the recipe to make the decorations – I used a silicone pig's face mould for mine.

You may notice that I haven't provided a pairing here, that's because with a pork pie the advice is 'what do you want to drink it with... ok, have that' – something I never thought I'd say, but I've yet to find something I don't like to eat pork pie with (but that might just say more about my relationship with pork pies than anything else!).

....

NOTE: Pretty much any classic British-style, or amber, beer with medium-low bitterness will work well here.

....

For the pastry:

750 g (1 lb 10 oz/6 cups) plain (all-purpose) flour, plus extra for dusting

1 teaspoon fine sea salt

1 tablespoon icing (confectioners') sugar

2 medium eggs in separate ramekins (custard cups), both whisked but one with a splash of water for egg wash

400 ml (13 fl oz/generous 1½ cups) cold water

300 g (10½ oz) lard, chopped into 4 cm (1½ in) cubes

Recipe method overleaf

Method

To make the jelly, put the bones and trotters in a large saucepan. Add just enough water to cover them, bring to the boil for a few minutes, and then discard the water.

Refill the pan with just enough water to come about 5 cm (2 in) above the meat. Bring back to the boil and then lower to a simmer. Add the rest of the jelly ingredients except the beer and beer chutney. Cover with a lid and simmer gently for about 2 hours.

Strain the liquid through a colander, add the beer and return to a gentle heat. Simmer until you have about 800 ml–1 litre (28 fl oz/ 3½ cups) of jellied stock. Stir in the beer chutney and set aside in a jug with a covering. (If you are not using it for a few hours, refrigerate, but you'll have to leave it out for about 2 hours for it to become liquid again before using.)

To make the filling, blitz the mace, allspice, salt and peppercorns in a spice grinder, then add the nutmeg. Dissolve the anchovy paste in the bitter and mix with the ground spices.

Take a quarter of the shoulder meat and half the hock meat and mince (grind) it with the bacon (you can ask your butcher to do this for you).

Mix the minced (ground) meat into the rest of the shoulder and hock and the rest of the filling ingredients, including the spice mix, and set aside.

To make the pastry, preheat the oven to 180°C (350°F/ Gas 4) and place a baking tray (sheet) large enough to accommodate the springform pan in the oven to heat. Get ready to work quickly!

Prepare a floured work surface, grab a rolling pin, flour the surface of that, and have your springform pan, a piece of dampened paper towel folded into a square, as well as a clean tea (dish) towel, a glass of cold water and a wooden spoon to hand.

Sift the flour, salt and icing sugar into a large, heatproof mixing bowl. Make a well in the flour and add the one of the eggs. Roughly stir them in, then make another well in the middle.

Place the bowl on the square of dampened paper towel to stop it slipping about during the next stage and have it close to the hob.

Put the water in a medium saucepan, add the lard and place over a medium heat before bringing to a vigorous, rolling boil.

Add the lard/water mix to the flour and mix very vigorously to combine as quickly as possible to form a pastry. Pour the glass of water into the saucepan over the lowest possible heat, take half the pastry out of the bowl and leave the rest in the heatproof bowl, placed over the saucepan and covered with a clean tea towel to keep warm.

Roll out half the pastry into a rough circle on a lightly floured surface to about 1.5 cm (⅝ in) thick and about 30–35 cm (12–14 in) wide.

Carefully roll it back onto the rolling pin and lift it gently into the prepared pan.

Using your knuckles, or the end of the rolling pin, press the pastry very gently into the base and base circumference of the tin and up the sides. Don't worry if you have some initial holes, just get it into shape and use little bits of overhanging pastry to patch the holes.

Fill your pie with the meat filling, packing it down lightly and making a slight mound in the middle, which will help support the lid.

Brush a little egg wash around the edge of the pastry case.

Take two-thirds of the remaining pastry and roll out a 1.5 cm (⅝ in) thick lid to fit the top of the pie and crimp it to the base with a fork (or, if you have crimping skills, use your fingers to make a traditional fluted crimp).

Egg-wash the top of the pie and make a small hole in the top. Push your digital thermometer into the centre of the pie through the hole and set it to 69°C (156°F) (the final cooked temperature should be 71°C (159°F) but it will continue to cook after you remove it from the oven).

Place the pie in the oven and turn it down to 160°C (325°F/Gas 3). (At this point, also turn the hob off under your bowl with the pastry in.) Cook for approximately 2 hours or until your digital thermometer beeps.

If you are going to decorate with pastry decorations (like in the photo), then make up a little flour glue with 1 tablespoon of flour and 1 teaspoon of water to attach them to the pie.

When your pie is cooked, remove from the oven (leaving it on) and allow to rest for 15–20 minutes.

Whilst that is resting, turn your remaining pastry

back out into the pan and gently heat it up again, beating it vigorously with a spoon.

Take three-quarters of it and mould it into whatever your chosen decoration is or push into silicone moulds. If doing the latter, put these in the oven for 15 minutes.

Return the remaining dough to keep warm over the pan of water as before.

Gently run a knife under the crimped edge of the pie, hard against the pan edge, to release any stuck bits and release the springform sides. Gently slide them off, leaving the pie on the pan base. Place on a wire cooling rack.

At this stage, pour just a tiny bit of your jelly into the hole at the top through a funnel and wait for a few minutes. It will give you a heads up about any leaks you may have, which you can plug by gently smoothing some of the remaining pastry into place with a palette or butter knife.

Once you've done this, egg – wash the whole of your pie, glue any decorations on, egg-wash again and put it back in the oven for 10 minutes.

At the 10-minute mark, egg-wash one last time and allow to cook for another 5 minutes.

Take the pie out of the oven, place back on the wire cooling rack and allow to cool for an hour. When the hour is almost up, take the jelly and check that it's liquid; if not, just heat gently until it is.

Get a couple of ice cubes out of the freezer and put them in a ramekin (custard cup) beside your pie and perhaps ask someone to come and be on standby in case you need any 'leak assistance'. Now, using a funnel, very slowly pour the remaining jelly into the pie. If your pie springs a leak anywhere, press an ice cube against it, and it should set the jelly quickly enough that it will plug the gap itself. Every time the jelly comes right up to the top, wait a few moments for it to settle down again and repeat until it no longer recedes. Place in the fridge.

All you need to do now is sit down with a well-earned beer and wait for a few hours until it's ready to scoff. This will keep for about a week and is great with either Beer Chutney (page 140) or Beer Mustard (page 136), or both!

Venison Beerguignon
Serves 6–8

Ingredients

2 × 330 ml (11¼ fl oz/ 1⅓ cups) bottles of Flanders red or Oud Bruin (see 'Cook' beers on page 85 for suggestions)

500 ml (17 fl oz/2 cups) bottle of smoked wheat beer (see 'Cook' beers on page 150 for suggestions)

335 ml (11¼ fl oz/1⅓ cups) bottle of strong dark Belgian ale (see 'Cook' beers on page 105 for suggestions)

1.5 kg (3 lb 5 oz) venison shin (or beef shin if you can't get venison), cut into 6 cm (2½ in) cubes, plus shank bones (ask your butcher to cut them in half lengthways or get 400 g (14 oz) marrow bones

3 fresh bay leaves

1 large bunch of thyme

3 sprigs of rosemary

1 tablespoon fine sea salt

8 tablespoons plain (all-purpose) flour

1 garlic bulb, separated into cloves and peeled

300 g (10½ oz) pancetta, diced into lardons (pieces)

500 g (1 lb 2 oz) pearl onions or small shallots, blanched and peeled

2 knobs of unsalted butter

1 tablespoon sugar

400 g (14 oz) small chestnut mushrooms, washed*

2 tablespoons mushroom ketchup

2 tablespoons English mustard powder

2–3 tablespoons red wine or dubbel beer vinegar (to your taste)

groundnut or rapeseed oil, for frying

fine sea salt

there is a myth about mushrooms 'absorbing water' or that 'you'll wash away the flavour' if you wash them, but this has been thoroughly disproved and saves you lots of time on tedious prep work with a little brush

Beef stew doesn't sound half as lush as boeuf bourguignon, does it? Those stupidly sexy French and their awesome language of love have it sewn up when it comes to making simple things sound alluring, so as a small measure of revenge I've decided to mess with one of France's favourite dishes and make it better – by using beer.

You'll need a deep, 30 cm- (12 in-) wide casserole dish or other ovenproof dish that can be covered with foil. To pair, choose any of strong Belgian dark ales or the Flanders red or Oud Bruin depending on your preference.

....

NOTE: I do this over 48 hours. You can do it in 24 hours (starting at the overnight step) but the flavour development, if you allow it that extra day, really is fantastic. It's well worth the effort to get ahead and it means you can relax with family and friends instead of racing around the kitchen.

....

Method

Day 1

In a large, non-metallic bowl, pour half a bottle of each beer in, stir then submerge the meat. Tie the bay leaves, thyme and rosemary together to make a bouquet garni. Bash them slightly to release the oils, then add it to the bowl with the salt. Leave to marinate in the fridge overnight.

Day 2

Take the venison out of the fridge half an hour before you're going to use it, fish the meat out and dry it gently on some paper towels but don't apply any pressure. Reserve the marinade.

Heat the oven to 120°C (250°F/Gas ½) and put a deep ovenproof dish in the oven.

Get a big ziplock bag and put the flour in it, add the venison, seal and shake until the meat is evenly covered. Set a colander over a bowl. Meanwhile, place a large frying pan (skillet) on a medium heat, and when it comes to temperature add about a 1 cm (½ in) depth of oil. Brown the meat in batches, without crowding the pan or you'll steam instead of getting that lovely Maillard reaction you're looking for. Transfer to the colander once it's browned.

When all the meat is browned, pour off any excess oil from the pan and check whether the pan just has browned bits or whether there's some burnt stuff in there. If it's the former, deglaze it with a little water and add it to the reserved marinade. If it's the latter, don't – it'll add an unpleasant bitterness to the final dish.

Take the dish out of the oven and put the meat into it, then add the meat juices from the bowl under the colander, and the bones. Add the bouquet garni and the whole garlic cloves (they go all sweet and slippery in the finished dish), then top up the dish with the other half bottle of smoked wheat beer and strong dark Belian ale, along with the reserved marinade. Put the lid on and cook in the oven for 3½–4 hours until the meat is just covered (top up with water, if necessary). Check the meat is tender, then leave to cool in its cooking liquid and refrigerate overnight.

Day 3

An hour before you're ready to serve, take the stew out of the fridge, lift off any excess fat on the top while it's still solidified and heat the oven to 140°C (275°F/Gas 1).

Take a large frying pan (skillet) and add a small amount of groundnut oil. Add the pancetta lardons and fry gently in the oil for 5–10 minutes until they start to brown, making sure they are slowly releasing their flavour and any fat on them is getting rendered nicely – place in a bowl and set aside.

Take the pearl onions or shallots, pop them in the pan and start to brown, which will take around 15–20 minutes; it just needs a little patience.

Return the pancetta to the pan with the onions, add a knob of butter and sprinkle the sugar over the top.

As the sugar starts to turn brown, add 2 tablespoons of the Flanders red or Oud Bruin, but be careful as it will sizzle and spit. As it turns into a caramel, swirl the lardons and onions well so you get a nice coating, then allow to cool slightly. Pour the lardons, onions and caramel into the venison dish.

Clean out the pan and fry the mushrooms in the remaining knob of butter until golden but still firm. For the last 10 seconds, pour in the mushroom ketchup and allow to reduce to get sticky and coat the mushrooms. Add them to the venison dish, gently stirring to combine.

Place the stew in the oven, turn down to 120°C (250°F/Gas ½) and cook for about an hour, without the lid, to allow the casserole to thicken.

Five minutes before you're ready to serve, add 150 ml (5 fl oz/scant ⅔ cup) of the Flanders red or Oud Bruin. Mix the mustard powder with the vinegar and stir through well, testing the sauce as you go for the right acidity. Check for seasoning and remove the shank bones and serve.

Ale-roast Goose with Double Red Cabbage
Serves 6–8

Ingredients

500 ml (17 fl oz/2 cups) smoked beer (see 'Cook' beers on page 150)

500 ml (17 fl oz/2 cups) strong dark Belgian ale (see 'Cook' beers on page 105)

500 ml (17 fl oz/2 cups) milk stout (see 'Cook' beers below)

2 tablespoons soft brown sugar

4.5–5.5 kg (10–11 lb) whole goose

2 long carrots

2 large celery sticks

1 onion, quartered

1 garlic bulb, broken into cloves but not skinned

8 black peppercorns

a good bouquet garni: bay leaves and your woody herbs of choice, such as sage, thyme, rosemary, oregano or marjoram

2 litres (70 fl oz/8 cups) good-quality chicken stock (if needed)

fine sea salt

30 ml (1 fl oz) Flanders red

Cook

It's difficult to dictate what to pair with the goose because it depends on whether you choose to cook it with the cabbage or something else, but, in general, any of the dark strong ale will work or, my preferred match, is a Flanders red or Oud Bruin, but they can be an acquired taste.

Big Smoke Milk Stout – UK

Left Hand Milk Stout – USA

Batch Brewing Elsie the Milk Stout – Australia

Cassels & Sons Milk Stout – New Zealand

Bristol Beer Factory Milk Stout – UK

Castle Milk Stout – South Africa

Just before you panic and think 'god, a goose, that's huge and expensive!' let me just say you can use a couple of ducks instead, if you want, as that's actually is how this dish started life; just use the same amount of ingredients, distributed equally between the two birds, or reduce the ingredients by half for just one.

And this isn't just for Christmas; it makes for a great entertaining dish too because it's basically make ahead and re-heat, freeing you up to spend more time with friends and family.

You can prepare both the bird and the cabbage up to three days in advance. In fact, the cabbage is better when it's had time to mature. And if you want to serve this with roast potatoes (why wouldn't you?) you will get far crispier ones by par-boiling them the day before and refrigerating them, making this probably – almost certainly – the most hassle-free feast you'll ever make.

You will need a very deep, very large roasting tray (pan) for this and some turkey foil.

Method

Preheat the oven to 120°C (250°F/Gas ½) and boil the kettle full of water.

Warm the beers in a saucepan and add the sugar.

Pierce the goose skin all over, paying special attention to the fat pockets around the legs. Put the goose on a trivet, put it in the sink and pour the kettle of hot water over it.

Make a square 'nest' for the goose with the carrots and celery in a large roasting tin (pan), then scatter the onions, garlic, pepper and bouquet garni in the middle and place the goose on top, breast-side up. Pour half the beer/sugar mixture over it and sprinkle lightly with fine salt, then turn breast-side down and repeat.

Add enough stock to the tin so the breast and most of the legs are covered (or as high as you dare, remembering you

have to take it out when it's hot!) and cook for 4–6 hours. When the leg bone starts to come away easily, it's done.

Take out of the oven and allow to cool for at least an hour, uncovered in the pan. Lift the goose out very carefully, making sure you empty the cavity of juices into the tin, but don't throw the juices away!

Put the goose on a plate to cool. Put any juices from resting back in tin, and put the goose in the refrigerator uncovered (if putting in a cold place like a garage, shed or larder instead, cover with muslin or something breathable).

Warm the roasting tin on the hob and scrape the bits off the bottom, then pass the liquid through a fine sieve into a tall and thin a receptacle that will accommodate the

Double Red Cabbage
Serves 8

Ingredients

1–1.25 kg (2 lb 4 oz–2 lb 12 oz) red cabbage

15 g (½ oz) unsalted butter

2 red onions, sliced into half moons

330 ml (11¼ fl oz/1⅓ cups) Flanders red or Oud Bruin (see 'Cook' beers on page 85 for suggestions)

50 ml (1¾ fl oz/scant ¼ cup) port

25 g (1 oz/¼ cup) sultanas (golden raisins)

1 Ceylon cinnamon stick

2 allspice berries

2 fresh bay leaves

grated zest and juice of 1 large orange

1 teaspoon red wine vinegar

fine sea salt

Method

Cut the cabbage in half, then quarters and then shred on the widest setting of a mandoline or by hand so that the slices are more than 2 cm (¾ in) thick.

Get a very large frying pan (skillet) or shallow pan, put over a medium-low heat, add the butter and gently fry the onions until they are yielding but not coloured.

Add the cabbage, two-thirds of the beer, the port, sultanas, cinnamon, allspice, bay leaves and orange zest. The liquid should just come to the underside of the cabbage, but if it doesn't, add a little water. Put a lid on the pan, very slightly ajar to let some steam out, turn down very low (use a pan heat diffuser if you have one) and allow to bubble away for 45 minutes.

At this stage you can allow to cool and put in the fridge (freeze the orange juice and remaining beer in a tub together).

When you're ready to serve, add the remaining beer and juice, allow to simmer down slightly. Just one minute before you're about to serve, season lightly with salt, stir that in and check that it tastes slightly under-seasoned. Remove from the heat, fish out the cinnamon stick, bay leaves and allspice berries, add the vinegar, stir and serve.

169

Recipe photo overleaf

---

liquid you can find. Press hard on the veg to extract all the flavour before discarding them. Allow the liquid to cool and then put it in the fridge overnight.

On the big day, take the goose out of the refrigerator just before you want to re-heat it and allow it to come to room temperature. Meanwhile, preheat the oven to 180°C (350°F/Gas 4). Sprinkle the breast and legs lightly with fine salt, then put the goose in the oven for 40 minutes or until you can stick a knife into the leg meat and take it out hot.

While the goose is re-heating, take the jug of cooking juices out of the fridge and there should now be a truly glorious layer of goose fat on top. Leave it to warm up for a few moments and then gently run a sharp knife around the edge of the jug to remove the fat, carefully, in a disc from the top. Use this for the roast potatoes.

Put the juices in a pan and reduce to your favoured consistency for gravy. It's smart to have some chicken stock, any leftover non-bitter beer or water on hand just in case you need more volume but it should enough. Add the Flanders red just before you are about to dish up.

Rest your goose, uncovered so the skin stays crisp, for about 10 minutes (although it will stay warmer for longer if you need a bit more time. If so, you could carve it and put it in a heated dish). Then serve it with red cabbage (above), roast potatoes and all the trimmings and yes, that means Brussels sprouts too in my world!

Recipe photo overleaf

Beer-brined Porchetta Stuffed with Rhubarb & Fennel
Serves 8–10

Ingredients

For the pork and brine:

75 g (2½ oz) fine sea salt

1.1 litres (38 fl oz/4⅔ cups) hand-warm water

400 ml (13 fl oz/generous 1½ cups) well-chilled Abbey-blonde ale

2 kg (4 lb 8 oz) pork loin (your loin needs to fit inside the belly with at least 5 cm/1¾ in to spare when rolled)

4 kg (8 lb 8 oz) boneless pork belly, skin on

For the stuffing and gravy:

60 g (2 oz) fennel bulb, finely chopped

6 garlic cloves, finely chopped

100 g (3½ oz) chopped onion (I use pre-chopped frozen for ease)

splash of groundnut, grapeseed or other neutral oil

80 g (3 oz) rhubarb (forced for preference), cut in 1 cm (½ in) slices

2 tablespoons finely chopped sage leaves

2 tablespoons finely chopped thyme leaves

3 tablespoons finely chopped parsley (feel free to include stems)

1 teaspoon fennel seeds

2 teaspoons chilli (hot pepper) flakes (or more depending on your preference for heat)

10 good grinds of black pepper

150 g (5 oz/3 cups) panko breadcrumbs

500 ml (17 fl oz/2 cups) chicken stock

1 tablespoon red miso paste

40 ml (13½ fl oz/scant ½ cup) Abbey-blonde ale, to finish the pan juices

There seems to be no way to make a small amount of porchetta, but the absolute joy is, once it's prepared and trussed, you can cut it into portions and freeze it, meaning you've got porky deliciousness on hand whenever you need it.

Start this the day before and it'll be a cinch to cook on the day. Perhaps enlist another pair of hands to help you truss the roast. I strongly recommend you get good pork from your butcher, who will also be able to cut everything to size for you.

You'll need a large roasting tin (pan) and an oven-safe digital thermometer probe.

Cook ⋯⋯ Pair ⋯⋯

Cook	Pair
Leffe Blonde – Belgium	La Trappe Tripel – Netherlands
Gouden Carolus – Belgium	Spencer Brewery Trappist Ale – USA
Ommegang Tripel Perfection – USA	Brasserie de la Senne Bruxellensis – Belgium
Mikkeller Trippel A – Denmark	Orval – Belgium
Adnams Tripel Knot – UK	Russian River Consecration – USA

Recipe method overleaf

To prepare the pork, stir the salt into the warm water in a non-metallic bowl until dissolved, then add the beer and chill for 15 minutes.

Slice the pork loin three-quarters of the way through lengthways and open it out like a book. Ensure the pork belly is unrolled if it's been trussed.

Take 2 large, shallow, non-metallic dishes and lay the unrolled belly, skin-side up, and pork loin in them. Pour the brine into the belly dish until it stops just short of the skin, then add the rest to the pork loin. Refrigerate overnight.

Take your pork out of the fridge an hour before you're ready to start preparing it on the day.

Preheat the oven to 140°C (275°F/Gas 1) and while it is heating up, make the stuffing and gravy.

Put the fennel, garlic, onions and oil in a frying pan (skillet) over a medium-low heat. Gently sweat until the garlic loses its raw smell and the onions and fennel are becoming translucent. Set aside to cool.

In a large mixing bowl, put the rhubarb, herbs, spices, breadcrumbs and 100 ml (3½ fl oz/scant ½ cup) of the brine, mix lightly and allow to rest for 5 minutes.

Add the cooked garlic, onion and fennel. Mix and stir well until you have almost

a paste; if it's not holding together add more of the remaining brine until it does.

Put a large chopping board with a double layer of paper towel underneath and another double layer on the surface of the board, and lay out 8 x 12 cm- (4½ in-) long lengths of butcher's twine, evenly spaced, on top of that.

Take the pork belly from the brine, allow it to drain, then lay it on the paper towel and string, skin side down.

Take a sharp knife and lightly score the belly meat, about 2 cm (¾ in) deep, in a diamond pattern and plaster three-quarters of the stuffing into the surface.

When that's done, take your butterflied pork loin from the brine, allow to drain, then place lengthways along one of the long edges of the pork belly. Put the rest of the stuffing in the middle of the loin and fold the loin back over to encase the stuffing. Reserve a few tablespoons of the brine for the gravy.

Working from the edge of the pork belly where the loin is, roll the belly tightly around the loin and then truss with your pieces of string (it's helpful to have someone help you with this, unless you are adept at butcher's knots, which I'm not!).

Place in a roasting tin (pan) and add the chicken stock. Push your digital thermometer into the middle

of the loin and set to 68°C (154°F). Place in the oven on the middle rack and roast for at least 4 hours, keeping an eye on the liquid level in the base every hour or so. Top with a bit more water if it has dried out.

When your digital thermometer goes off, turn the oven up to 200°C (400°F/ Gas 6) and allow another 15 minutes cooking, making sure there's still at least 3 cm (1¼ in) of liquid in the bottom of the pan. Keep an eye on it as the last thing you want is for that luscious crackling to burn.

When your crackling is nice and crisp, turn the oven off, and crack open the oven door and allow to rest for half an hour.

When you're ready to serve, lift the roast pork onto your carving board.

Take the pan out of the oven and set it over a hob with a saucepan to one side.

Add the miso and a few tablespoons of the brine and scrape all the good stuff off the bottom of the pan, strain into the saucepan, add the beer and allow to reduce a bit whilst you carve.

You can either slice the pork up and stuff it into some buns with apple sauce, a drizzle of pan juice gravy and some rocket (arugula) or serve with roast potatoes and vegetables for a slap-up Sunday lunch.

Beeramisu

Serves 6

Ingredients

For the Savoiardi biscuit horns:

Makes 8 (you only need six but they're a bit fiddly so it pays to have insurance!)

4 eggs, separated

125 g (4 oz/scant ¾ cup) caster (superfine) sugar

½ teaspoon vanilla bean paste

50 g (2 oz/scant ½ cup) cornflour (cornstarch)

100 g (3½ oz/heaped ¾ cup) plain (all-purpose) flour

4 tablespoons icing (confectioners') sugar

For the filling:

250 ml (9 fl oz/1 cup) double (heavy) cream

250 g (9 oz) mascarpone

80 ml (2 fl oz/5 tablespoons) coffee liqueur

170 ml (6 fl oz/¾ cup) coffee stout

80 g (3 oz/⅔ cup) icing (confectioners') sugar

½ teaspoon vanilla bean paste

pinch of fine sea salt

For the chocolate soil:

100 g (3½ oz/heaped ½ cup) caster (superfine) sugar

2 tablespoons coffee beer, plus a further 100 ml (3½ fl oz/½ cup) for assembling

¼ teaspoon coffee liqueur, plus a further 2 teaspoons for assembling

75 g (2½ oz) dark chocolate, at least 70% cocoa solids, broken into tiny pieces

This recipe was inspired by the best cook with beer I know – a guy called Tim Wareman who heads up 'cause BEER loves FOOD in Amsterdam. One evening he cooked me a bespoke meal from a teeny tiny kitchen and I was utterly blown away. I knew immediately that we were kindred spirits and I can't recommend visiting his restaurant enough. He was kind to share how he makes his beeramisu with me and I have, in turn, put my own spin on it.

You don't have to make the biscuit horns, you can just make lady fingers biscuits. You'll just need to double the cornflour (cornstarch) and assemble like you would a traditional tiramisu, topping with the chocolate soil.

Method

First make the bicuits. Line a flat baking tray (sheet) with a silicone baking sheet or baking parchment. Prepare a piping bag with a round nozzle and place it in a large glass or stein. Heat the oven to 160°C (325°F/Gas 3).

Beat the egg yolks in a bowl with half the caster sugar and the vanilla paste.

Using a stand mixer or electric whisk, beat the egg whites until fluffy, then gradually whisk in the remaining sugar and the cornflour until you have shiny meringue that will hold a stiff peak.

Add the yolks to the egg whites with the flour, folding both of these things in gently with a rubber spatula. Spoon the mixture into the piping bag.

Pipe 2 (roughly) 15 cm (6 in) diameter circles onto your silicone mat on the baking sheet by starting with a blob in the middle and spiralling outwards.

Bake on the middle shelf of the oven for 8 minutes.

Using a palette knife, loosen from the sheet and then, carefully, roll around a cream horn mould that's been lightly sprayed with quick release spray to form a cone. Don't worry if they split slightly, push them back together gently, dust lightly with icing sugar and return to the oven on the baking tray for 4–5 minutes with the moulds still inside, or until they are a light golden colour and just crisping up. Allow to cool for a few minutes, then slide the moulds out.

Repeat another 3 times or until you have 6 cones – at this point you can use the spare batter to make ordinary lady finger biscuits. Just fold in 2 tablespoons of extra cornflour and dust them with icing sugar before you bake them.

. . . .

NOTE: Don't be tempted to try and do these all at once unless you have many cream horn moulds and many hands. You need the biscuits to be warm when you roll them or they'll just break apart.

. . . .

Recipe method continued overleaf

SPECIALIST EQUIPMENT:

silicone baking sheet

quick-release cake tin spray

cream horns moulds

piping bag with a round nozzle

cream siphon

TIP: If you don't have a cream siphon, use a piping bag fitted with a round nozzle to pipe the cream into the cones.

Method

To make the filling, whisk all the filling ingredients together in a bowl until firm.

Put in a piping bag without a nozzle (pinch the end closed with a clip or elastic band as you fill it), then squeeze into a cream siphon. Charge the siphon, shake extremely vigorously until the contents don't move any more and place in the fridge.

To make the chocolate soil, put the sugar, beer and coffee liqueur in a saucepan and place either a sugar thermometer or a digital temperature probe in the pan. Heat to 130°C (266°F).

Add the chocolate and whisk until it resembles soil texture. This may take anything from 2–7 minutes, depending on how strong the beer is and the type of chocolate.

Get your serving dish and make a semi-circle of chocolate soil in each one. Reserve about a fifth of the soil.

Mix together the extra coffee beer and coffee liqueur in a shallow bowl wide enough to fit the cones in lengthways.

If the thinner ends of your cones have a sizeable hole in them, break up some of your spare biscuit and dip briefly in the beer/coffee liqueur mix and gently push it into the narrow end to plug the gap.

Take the siphon from the fridge and shake vigorously once more, turn the siphon upside down, spray a little of the filling on a plate.

Dip the wide end of the biscuit cones in the beer/liqueur mix, and then in the plate of filling. Sprinkle with chocolate soil until the edges are coated, then fill the cones with the cream/mascarpone mix.

Finally, dip the edge where the join in the cone is in the beer/liqueur mix and place at right angles to the chocolate soil on your plate.

Cook .... Pair

Cook	Pair
Magic Rock Common Grounds – UK	Jolly Pumpkin Calabaza Blanca – USA
Innocence Brewing Midnight Roast – Hong Kong	Feral White – Australia
Mikkeller Beer Geek Breakfast – Denmark	Magic Rock Salty Kiss – UK
Meantime Coffee Porter – UK	Saison Dupont – Belgium
Left Hand Brewing Hard Wired Nitro – USA	Gulpener Korenwolf – Netherlands

Rhubarb & Matcha Green Tea
Serves 2–4

Ingredients

For the meringue swirls:

¼ teaspoon red food colouring gel (it's really important it's gel, not liquid)

6 drops sweet orange oil

1½ tablespoons vanilla bean paste

2 large egg whites

50 g (2 oz/heaped ¼ cup) caster (superfine) sugar

50 g (2 oz/heaped ⅓ cup) icing (confectioners') sugar

For the ice cream:

280 ml (9½ fl oz/generous 1 cup) buttermilk

100 ml (3½ fl oz/scant ½ cup) well-chilled rhubarb sour beer

5 tablespoons maple syrup

1 teaspoon matcha green tea, plus 2 teaspoons to sprinkle over the top

pinch of fine sea salt

For the poached rhubarb:

400 g (14 oz) forced rhubarb (save the off-cuts for the liquid gel later in recipe)

1 tablespoon Belgian wheat beer or rhubarb sour beer (see 'Cook' beers on page 65 for examples of Belgian wheat beer)

¼ teaspoon vanilla bean paste

1 tablespoon maple syrup

For the liquid gel:

150 ml (5 fl oz/scant ⅔ cup) rhubarb beer

45 g (1¾ oz/¼ cup) caster (superfine) sugar

½ teaspoon agar agar

knife-point of red food colouring gel

I love rhubarb. You may have noticed because this is the second recipe it's turned up in, which is just as well because you often have to buy it in about the same amounts as both the porchetta and this recipe call for … are you thinking flashy lunch and dessert too?

This does require some skill but mostly it requires patience. Putting all the parts together takes time but what I've done is make it over a few days, as I've been waiting for other things to cook or if I've got a bit of time to kill, and it's worked out quite nicely.

You'll also need a small paint brush or a clean make-up brush. If rhubarb isn't in season, then you could easily substitute strawberries or maybe apricots or peaches and use the corresponding beer flavours – experiment, have fun with it and enjoy sharing the leftover little meringues with people too.

Cook & Pair

Any of these beers will go well with the dish, and if you want to change out the rhubarb for another fruit then by all means do, just correspond the fruit in the beer.

Ilkley Brewery Siberia – UK

Brasserie St Germain Rhub'IPA – France

The Bruery Ruebarb – USA

Thornbridge Rhubarb de Saison – UK

Brick Brewery Rhubarb Sour – UK

Brouhaha Brewery Strawberry & Rhubarb – Australia

SPECIALIST EQUIPMENT:

disposable piping bag with a star-shaped nozzle

sous vide

ruler or measuring tape

Recipe method overleaf

First make the meringue swirls. Prepare a large disposable piping bag with a star-shaped nozzle, and turn it inside out.

In a bowl, mix together the red food colouring gel, orange oil and vanilla paste. Paint 2 stripes of it up the inside of the icing bag, leave for a bit to dry slightly, then repeat (over the same lines) three more times.

Carefully turn the bag the right way out and place in a tall pint glass or stein, folded over the edge of the glass, ready for filling.

Preheat the oven to 110°C (225°F/ Gas ¼) or its lowest setting.

Line 2 baking trays (sheets) with 2 pieces of baking parchment cut to the same size.

Using a stand mixer or electric whisk, whisk the egg whites until they stand in firm, white peaks. Add the sugar one tablespoon at a time, ensuring it's well incorporated each time. Remove the whisk and add half the icing sugar, folding it in with a rubber spatula, then repeat.

Gently spoon the meringue mixture into the piping bag. Dot 4 bits of meringue on each corner of the baking tray, stick the baking parchment to them and press down lightly. Now time for the swirls: squeeze the bag gently and pipe a small blob of meringue – the colour may take a few seconds to come through but it will eventually.

Keep doing this in rows, with each blob about 2.5 cm (1 in) apart until you run out of mixture. Bake for 18–20 minutes, turning your tray halfway through. If any start to crack then take the tray

out immediately. Remove from the oven, allow to cool, then put in a sealed plastic tub until needed. They will keep for up to a week.

To make the ice cream, whisk together all the ingredients in a bowl, then place in the ice-cream maker to churn. Freeze in a sealable tub when done. If you don't have an ice-cream maker, put into a container in the freezer. Stir every 30 minutes to break up the ice crystals until fully frozen.

Prepare the poached rhubarb. Preheat the sous vide to 61°C (140°F).

Take a cleaned measuring tape or metal ruler and lay it along the side of the cutting board and take one piece of the pinkest bit of rhubarb, trim the ends and then trim down to 8 cm (3¼ in).

This is the guide piece. Use the 'guide' piece of rhubarb to cut 12 pieces of as equal width as you can manage. (Reserve all the off-cuts as you will need them for the gel.) Then cut each even strip into 3 cm- (1¼ in-) wide pieces. You should end up with 24 pretty even pieces.

Get the sous vide bag and arrange the rhubarb pieces in a row at the bottom; you want them to fit snugly. If they don't all fit, just use another bag and re-work the dimensions so they are snug.

Pop the beer, vanilla paste and syrup in a small bowl, whisk together, then pour into the bag with the rhubarb. Vacuum seal the bag, being careful not to suck all the liquid out, and pop in the sous vide for 35 minutes.

Take out, dry the bag and refrigerate or freeze until needed.

....

NOTE: If you don't have a sous vide then you can put the ingredients in a heavy zip-lock bag, gently squeezing all the air out as you seal it. Secure with elastic bands and poach in just below simmering water for 10–15 minutes depending on thickness. It should just yield to the touch.

....

To make the liquid gel, put all the ingredients in a saucepan, plus 150 g (5 oz) of the reserved rhubarb off-cuts. Bring to a vigorous simmer for 3 minutes and then lower to a gentle simmer for another 10 minutes.

Pour into a bowl and pop in the freezer or fridge until set into a solid gel, then spoon the gel into a blender and blitz until utterly smooth and bright pink. Decant into a squeezy bottle and refrigerate.

To assemble, remove all the dessert components out of the cupboard, fridge or freezer.

Take 4 large serving plates. Gently slide the pieces of rhubarb out of the bag and arrange 6 pieces on the centre of each plate, as shown in the recipe photo. Gently, using the squeezy bottle, dot some gel around the rhubarb. Place the meringue swirls by the gel, in a pretty pattern. Carefully quenelle your ice cream and slide gently onto the rhubarb. Sprinkle a line of matcha green tea across the plate then rush to the table to serve – it melts quite quickly!

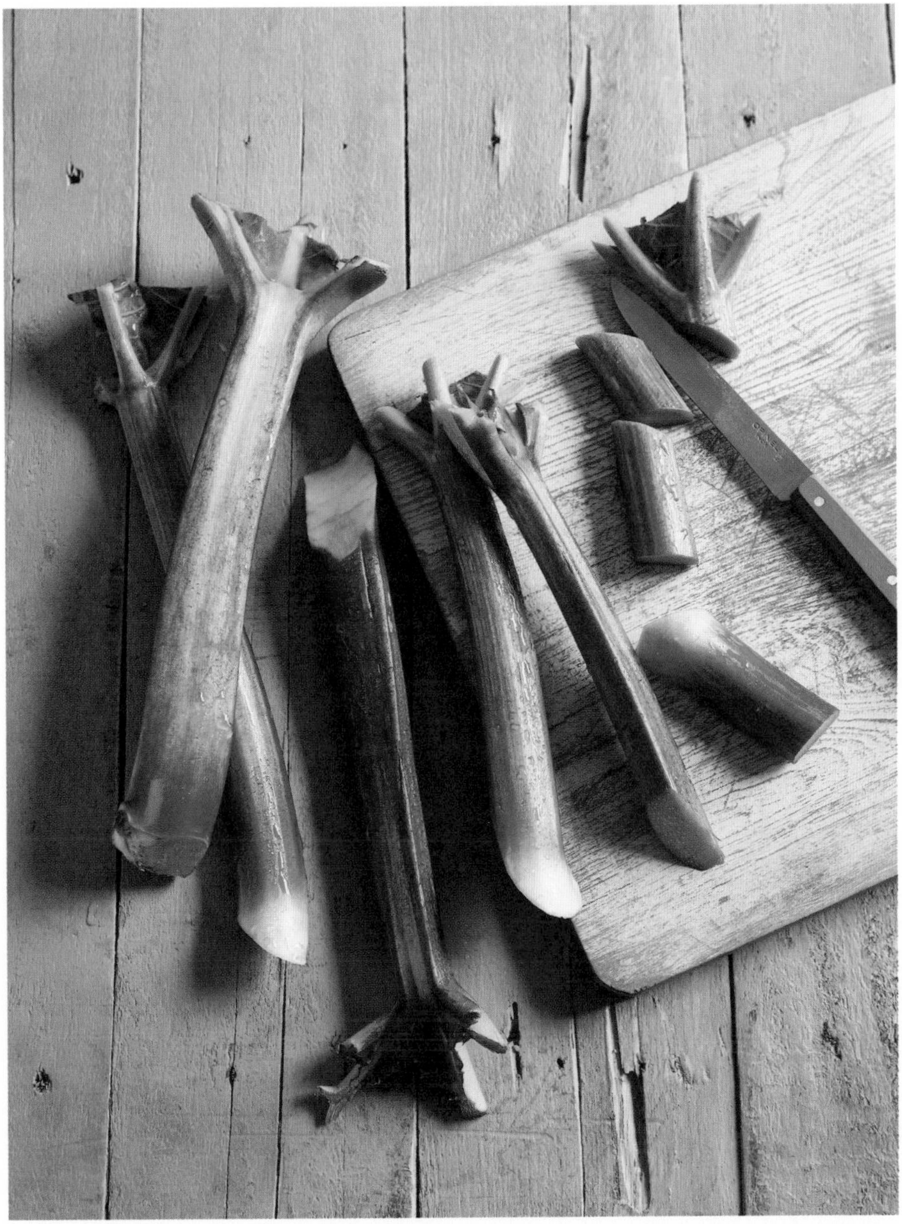

Lambic Marshmallows with Imperial Stout Fondue

Makes 24 marshmallows

Ingredients

For the marshmallows:

330 g (11½ oz) dark fruit lambic

22 g (scant 1 oz) powdered gelatine

1 g (scant ½ oz) agar agar

450 g (1 lb/2½ cups) caster (superfine) sugar

160 g (5½ oz) golden (or light corn) syrup

a few drops of red food colouring (optional)

groundnut or grapeseed oil, to grease

2 tablespoons cornflour (cornstarch)

2 tablespoons icing (confectioners') sugar

2 tablespoons sherbet (optional)

For the imperial stout chocolate fondue:

50 g (2 oz) imperial stout

50 g (2 oz) golden caster (superfine) sugar

200 g (7 oz) 70% dark chocolate with cocoa solids, broken into pieces

25 g (1 oz) maple syrup

SPECIALIST EQUIPMENT:

temperature probe or sugar thermometer

stand mixer, fitted with a balloon whisk

I've had a long love affair with marshmallows, particularly toasted around a camp fire and I both had a good laugh and a little cry when I was doing some clearing out recently because I found the transcript of a speech from my old Guide leader, Mrs Sear.

It was from when I was awarded my Baden Powell badge (the highest award you can get in the Girl Guides). It was peppered throughout with references to 'marshmallow crises'. Basically, if anything went wrong, my response to it was to start a fire and grab a bag of marshmallows. If only life was still so simple!

I also need to thank my marshmallow guru, Cheryl Black. She taught me how to make them and her S'mores made with bourbon marshmallows and chocolate-covered bacon are the stuff of legend.

Cook .... Pair

Pairing depends on how much of a chocoholic you are. If you are a massive one opt for the stouts, if not opt for the sharp fruit beers.

Cook Marshmallows:

Elgood's Coolship Fruit – UK

Funkwerks Raspberry Provincial – USA

Hanssens Oud Kriek – Belgium

3 Fonteinen Framboos – Belgium

Boatrocker Wildeberry – Australia

Cook Fondue:

Brasserie de Quercorb Montsegur – France

Birrificio del Ducato Verdi Imperial Stout – Italy

Ninkasi Vanilla Oatis – USA

Old Chimney's Good King Henry – UK

Alesmith Speedway Stout – USA

Method

First make the marshmallows. Fit the balloon whisk to a stand mixer.

Weigh 120 g (4 oz) of the beer and pour into the stand mixers bowl. Sprinkle with the gelatine and agar agar, then attach safely to the mixer.

Put the sugar and golden syrup in a large, deep saucepan (this will bubble up aggressively) and top up with the rest of the fruit lambic – this should cover the mixture once stirred, but top up with a little water if required.

Heat your temperature probe or sugar thermometer in the pan and bring to a boil. Do not walk away; this needs watching like a hawk or it will boil over.

Once the temperature hits 135°C (275°F), set the mixer on the lowest speed and start feeding the hot sugar mix into the bowl.

Add food colouring, if using, and, slowly and carefully, turn the speed up on the mixer until it's about two-thirds to maximum and leave to mix for 5–8 minutes.

Meanwhile, line a container that's roughly 12 × 8 cm (4½ × 3¼ in), with a piece of cling film (plastic wrap) about as long as your arm. (It needs to be bigger than your container so don't worry about it over hanging.) Lightly oil the cling film.

Check on your marshmallow mixture. After 5–8 minutes you'll get a kind of shiny, stretched bubble gum effect on the surface. Pour the mixture into the container and fold the overhanging cling film over the top. Pop the marshmallow mixture somewhere cool and leave to set for a couple of hours.

Put the cornflour, icing sugar and sherbet, if using, in a large bowl and mix.

When the marshmallow is fully set, gently peel the cling film away and, with an oiled knife, cut bite-size pieces and pop them in the large bowl, tossing them in the cornflour-sugar mix as you go so they don't stick together.

These will keep in a sealed container for about a week.

To make the fondue, put the imperial stout and sugar in a saucepan and gently heat for 5–8 minutes until all the sugar has dissolved and it becomes a light syrup. Do not allow to boil.

Melt the chocolate in a heatproof bowl over a simmering pan of water. Alternatively, heat in microwave, in short sharp bursts, stirring and repeating, until melted.

Stir the maple syrup into the melted chocolate, then stirring firmly but not too briskly, slowly add the beer syrup until you have the desired consistency for dipping. (The mixture should ribbon back into the pot when lifted with a spoon).

Put in a heated bowl or fondue in the middle of the table with long skewers for the marshmallows and get dunking!

Recipe photo overleaf

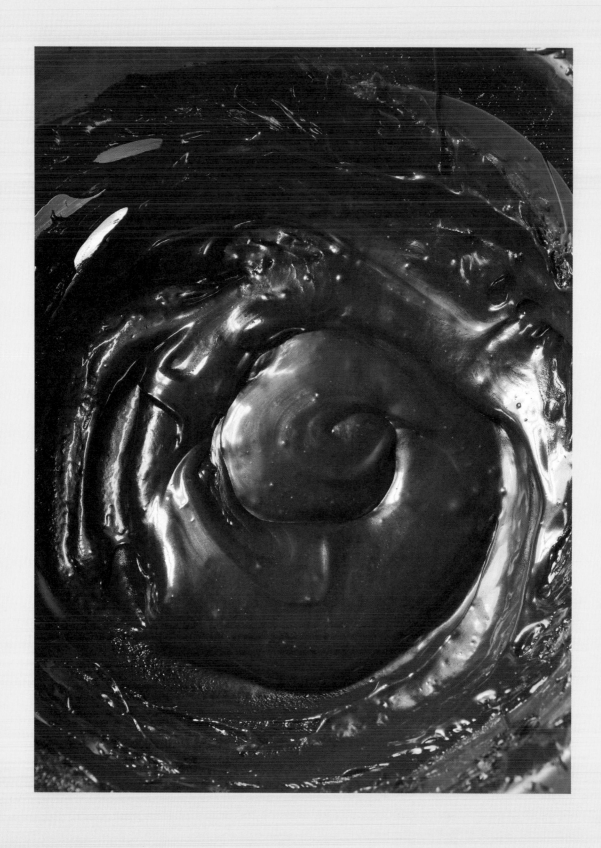

Orange Beer Ice Cream with Beery Chocolate Tart

Makes about 1.5 litres (52 fl oz/6 cups) ice cream

Ingredients

For the ice cream:

400 ml (13 fl oz/generous 1½ cups) whole (full-fat) milk

75 g (2½ oz) citrus pale ale (see 'Cook' beers on page 124)

300 ml (10 fl oz/1¼ cups) double (heavy) cream

5 egg yolks

140 g (4½ oz/heaped ¾ cup) golden caster (superfine) sugar

grated zest of 2 oranges

4 tablespoons of orange juice (blood orange if in season), frozen

For the pastry:

100 g (3½ oz/scant 1 cup) plain (all-purpose) flour, plus extra for dusting

50 g (2 oz/⅓ cup) icing (confectioners') sugar

50 g (2 oz) chilled unsalted butter, cubed

1 large egg yolk

1 tablespoon very cold water

For the filling:

110 g (3½ oz) unsalted butter

100 g (3½ oz) dark chocolate with 90% cocoa solids, broken into shards

50 g (2 oz) dark chocolate with chilli with 70% cocoa solids, broken into shards

50 ml (1¾ fl oz/scant ¼ cup) coffee beer (see 'Cook' beers on page 62)

150 g (5 oz/heaped ¾ cup) golden caster (superfine) sugar

75 g (2½ oz/scant ⅔ cup) plain (all-purpose) flour

6 medium eggs

The tart is a classic recipe. It just has a few small beery tweaks that I think really enhance the depth of the chocolate flavour and also there's science here in that the presence of ethanol creates a small amount of destabilisation in the chocolate, which means it's a little more forgiving in the cooking stakes. The beer keeps it slightly gooey, which is really the joy of it.

Method

To make the ice cream, gently heat the milk, beer and cream in a sauceoan, until it starts to just bubble.

In a large bowl, whisk together the egg yolks and sugar until very pale then gradually whisk in the warm cream mixture. Do not stop whisking or you'll get lumps.

Return to the pan, gently heat, and stir until thickened. Remove from the heat and allow to cool for a few moments and then vigorously stir in the orange zest and frozen juice, which will help bring the temperature down. Pass the mixture through a fine sieve (in case you did scramble some egg) into a bowl and allow to chill in fridge.

Once the mixture is chilled, churn in an ice-cream maker or freeze in a freezer container, stirring every half an hour to break up the ice crystals.

To make the pastry, put the flour and icing sugar in a food processor and pulse. Add in the butter, a few cubes at a time, and pulse before adding in the egg yolk. Pulse until it's starting to amalgamate and then add the water and pulse until it comes together in a ball. Add more water if the mixture is too dry.

Put the pastry dough on a lightly floured surface and quickly knead it together until smooth. Wrap in cling film (plastic wrap) and leave to rest in fridge for an hour.

Preheat the oven to 200°C (400°F/Gas 6) and grease a 28 cm (11 in) tart tin. Roll out the chilled pastry on a floured work surface, as thin as you can and drape over your tart tin, pressing the pastry into the sides. Shave off any excess pastry and place in the fridge for 30 minutes. Reserve any spare pastry in the fridge.

Once the pastry case is chilled, prick the base with a fork, cover with baking parchment, top with baking beans and blind bake in the oven for about 5–8 minutes until lightly golden. Check for holes and patch if needed. Allow to cool while you are making the filling.

For the filling, melt the butter in a pan over a low heat. Add the chocolate shards and beer and then stir until smooth. Remove from heat and add the sugar and flour, then beat in the eggs one at a time.

Put the cooked pastry case on a baking tray (sheet), pour in the chocolate mixture. Give it a few gentle taps to clear any bubbles, then bake for 10–12 minutes, turning halfway through to ensure even cooking. It should be set but slightly wobbly in the middle. Once cooked, remove from the oven and allow to cool, before slicing and serving with a scoop of orange ice cream.

SAY CHEESE!

Cheese and beer are the most perfect of partners, it may sound odd as we are always told about cheese and wine but, trust me, try it and you'll never look back.

Cheese with beer. It's a pretty bold statement, isn't it? Surely decades of wine and cheese parties can't be wrong but I'm afraid that they very much are.

And I say this with such confidence because when I'm working with particularly recalcitrant sommeliers, I'll often challenge them to pick four wines to go with four cheeses of their choice from their cheese board and then I bring in beers and we test them on both the front and back of house staff. I've not lost yet, although there have been a few close-run face-offs where the sommeliers have brought out some pretty pricey wines in an attempt to beat me. Nice try, chaps – beer is always going to come out best.

Secondly, there are a number of taste, flavour and sensory aspects to beer that help it pip wine to the post, most of the time:

1. High water content: helps refresh the palate.

2. CO₂: that sparkle helps scrub the tongue clean, allowing you to enjoy every bit anew.

3. Grain base: what do we always pair with cheese? Grain-based products like bread and crackers. The flavour combinations make sense in your head.

4. Range of available flavour profiles in beer: beer actually has a larger 'flavour wheel' than wine, which makes sense when you think it already has more base ingredients, a wider range of fermentation profiles and often has what are known as 'adjuncts', which just means added ingredients like fruits and spices.

5. Generally lower in alcohol content: ethanol (alcohol) will separate the lipids (fats) from the cheese, creating a film in the mouth, so a lower alcohol content drink is a better pairing.

There's also a third aspect to all this, which is: good, even great, beer is normally cheaper and easier to experiment with than half-decent wine, meaning you can find your perfect pairings at home without an enormous outlay, although I have offered you some thoughts on my favourite pairings on page 197.

Basic Principles of Cheese Pairing

The first thing I'm going to say is, remember your palate is personal. There are few hard and fast rules that can apply to everyone but years of experience, and a thankfully low cholesterol count, have allowed me to experiment with hundreds of different pairings. Here are some of the things I've found to be universally true – some of them are slightly more out there in terms of partnerships but I love them nonetheless.

1. Pair level of intensity with level of intensity: I know I've said this before but it bears repeating here, in particular. If you try and put an imperial stout with a young goat's cheese then your beer is going to stomp all over your cheese. Think English-style golden ale or a crisp pilsner.

2. Texture: this applies to both your beer and your food. Lower fat cheeses benefit from a more softly carbonated beer style, whereas fattier ones cry out for a more brisk bubbliness.

3. Finish on the cheese: it's not always about the style. Is the cheese rolled in ash? Well then, you don't want too smoky a beer or it'll be unpleasantly burnt-tasting. Is the rind washed? Well then, it's probably going to be quite stinky and earthy, so you want to counterpoint that with something fresh and vibrant. Is it herb-finished? Maybe look for a beer that has both complementary and similar flavours: perhaps a citrusy beer with a herbal edge.

4. Be bold: some of the most surprising matches have been when I've thrown caution to the wind and decided to try something a bit off piste. For example, a very low bitterness NEIPA is a surprisingly good match for an Epoisse and a gueuze can go very well with a slightly creamy blue cheese.

5. Fun with friends: this journey of discovery is something that works incredibly well with friends, nominating everyone to bring three beers and three cheeses to a gathering and everyone digging in and experimenting is an absolute joy.

My Personal
Top 10

Beer & Cheese Pairings

01
Young goat's cheese with English-style golden ale or good-quality lager

02
Feta with New England-style IPA

03
Havarti/Munster/Port Salut-style cheese with English-style IPA

04
Mature Cheddar with English-style mild

05
Parmesan/Pecorino with Flanders Bruin

06
Brie/Camembert-style cheeses with Saison

07
Stilton or similar blue cheese with Barley wine

08
Epoisse/Stinking Bishop/ honking rind-washed cheese with Imperial stout

09
Soft blue cheese like Gorgonzola with gueuze

10
Aged Gouda-style cheese with old ale or Belgian quadrupel

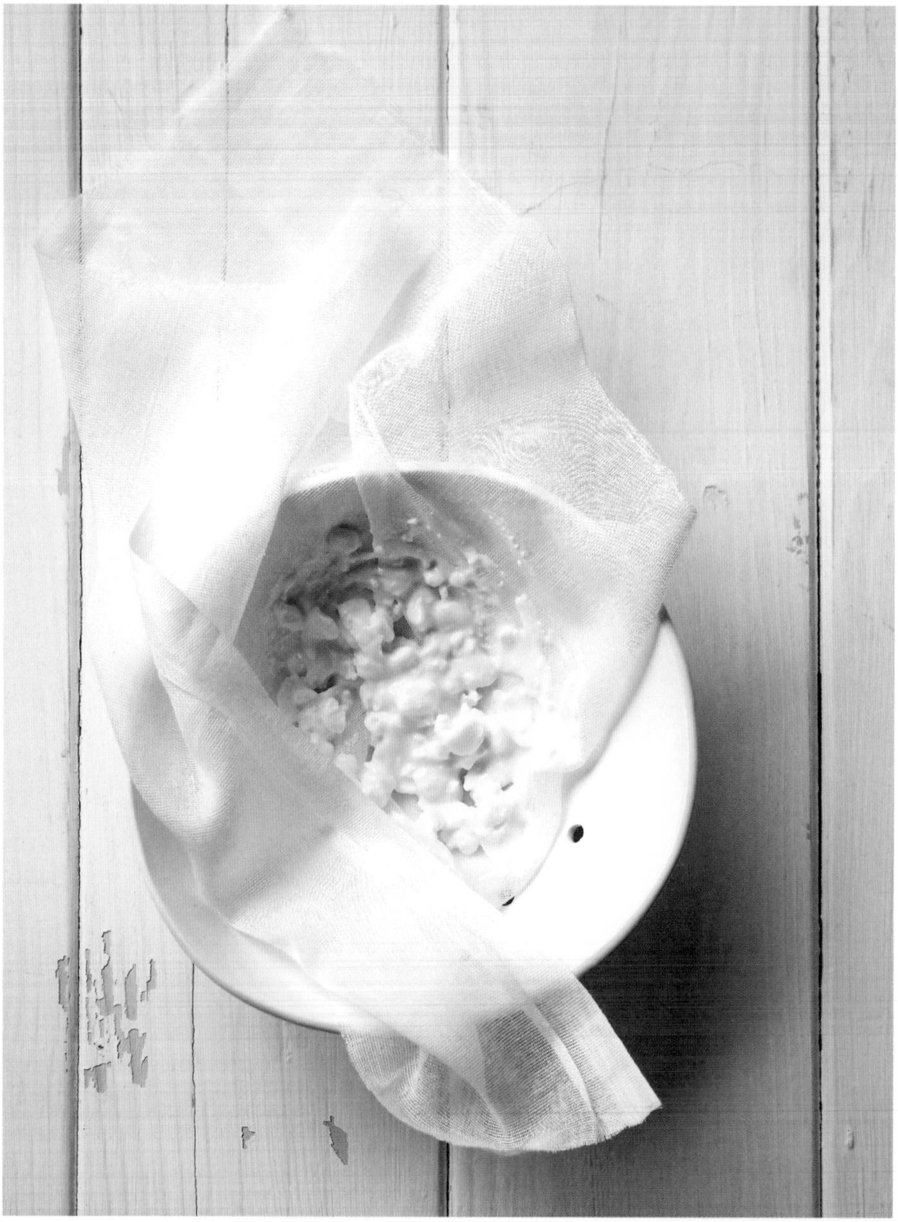

Berliner Weisse/Gose Cottage Cheese
Makes 300–350 g (10–12 oz)

Ingredients

2.25 litres (76 fl oz/9 cups) whole (full-fat) milk

330 ml (11¼ fl oz/1⅓ cups) Berliner weisse or gose, at room temperature

fine sea salt

Cook & Pair

You can use any of these for either the cooking or the pairing aspect – enjoy!

Westbrook Gose – USA

Magic Rock Salty Kiss – UK

10 Barrel Cucumber Crush – USA

Berliner Kindl – Germany

Wayward Brewing Sourpuss – Australia

8 Wired Brewing Cucumber Hippy – New Zealand

Original Ritterguts Gose – Germany

Mikkeller Drink'In Berliner – Denmark

Dugges Tropic Thunder – Sweden

Cervejaria Narcose Flip Flops to Heaven – Brazil

This idea had been kicking around in my brain for ages. I figured that if lemon juice or vinegar could do the job of separating curds from whey then why couldn't a pretty acidic beer? Turns out it will, you just need a bit more of it.

Sure, it doesn't yield masses but it has a super-lactic tang that seriously sharpens up the taste buds and you can play around with it as well, use goat's milk if you want an earthier tang, add spices or herbs, or even make it sweet or use colourings if you like. It's your gateway into cheese making.

The beer you use is up to the results you want to yield. For a sweeter version, use either dry hopped or sweet fruited. Want a really sour tangy result? Use a sour fruited one like gooseberry or rhubarb.

You need some fine muslin (cheesecloth) and either a sugar thermometer or a temperature probe for this.

....

NOTE: Do not throw the whey away (it's so much fun to type that). Pop it in the freezer for future use. It's full of enzymes so it's brilliant for using in marinades for tough cuts of meat, to use in pot roasts like pork in milk or even to replace the liquid element in bread.

....

Method

Heat the milk slowly in a saucepan to between 73–78°C (163–172°F), stirring from time to time so it's evenly heated.

When you hit that temperature, turn the heat right down and add the beer in four parts, stirring gently as you go. You should see the curds and whey separating.

Turn off the heat and allow to stand for 30 minutes.

Meanwhile, line a colander or sieve with a fine muslin (cheesecloth). When the 30 minutes is up, strain the curds, salt lightly and leave to firm up for another 30 minutes.

Refrigerate until you're ready to use. It will keep in the fridge sealed for about a week.

....

TIP: You can also turn this into paneer – all you need to do is twist the muslin into a tight flat puck shape and weigh it down with a weight for a few hours.

....

Beer Cheese Soup
Serves 4

Ingredients

200 g (7 oz) carrots, diced

250 g (9 oz) leek, trimmed, washed and diced

200 g (7 oz) celery sticks, diced

4 garlic cloves, smashed and finely chopped

700 ml (24 fl oz/scant 3 cups) brown chicken stock

500 g (1 lb 2 oz) Batsmans XXXB (or any of the 'Cook' beers below)

75 g (2½ oz) butter

40 g (1½ oz/⅓ cup) plain (all-purpose) flour

950 ml (32 fl oz/3¾ cups) whole (full-fat) milk

1 whole nutmeg, to grate

680 g (1 lb 8 oz) strong, extra mature Cheddar, grated, plus extra to garnish

1 tablespoon Worcestershire sauce

½ teaspoon English mustard powder★

hot sauce of choice or cayenne pepper (optional, I like Cholula)

fine sea salt and freshly ground black pepper

crusty bread, to serve

★ mustard powder is a great double duty store-cupboard ingredient, you can use it in all sorts of things like rubs, macaroni cheese and the like, or just mix with water – or beer – to knock up the perfect condiment without taking up further space in the fridge or cupboard

This is simplicity itself for when it's freezing cold outside, you're feeling poorly or if you've spent a good few hours exercising and have a calorie hole that needs filling. Or just because you've got loads of spare cheese in the fridge – any of these things are valid reasons for making beer cheese soup because it rocks!

As long as at least half of your cheese is a strong Cheddar then any melty cheese can be substituted, I find this a really good way to use up odds and ends of cheese.

Any of the beers suggested in the 'Cook' box on page 87 would pair beautifully with this soup.

Method

Heat a large saucepan over medium heat. Add the carrots, leek, celery and let them soften in their juices. Add the garlic and stir for another minute or so.

Deglaze the pan with the chicken stock, then remove from the heat. Allow it to settle to a simmer then add the beer. Return the pan to the heat and simmer gently for 8–10 minutes, until the vegetables are totally tender and the beer smell has settled into that fresh bread aroma.

Remove from the heat, blitz until smooth and set aside. (If you want a super-silky consistency, then pass through a fine sieve and muslin.)

In another saucepan, combine the butter and flour over a low heat to make a roux. Cook for 1 minute, then gradually whisk in the milk. Bring to the boil to make béchamel, stirring and whisking until thickened. Add a couple of gratings of nutmeg and then slowly whisk in the beer mixture until it's completely combined.

Slowly add the cheese, stirring until the whole lot is lusciously amalgamated.

In a small bowl, whisk together the Worcestershire sauce and mustard powder. Pour into the soup and whisk. Add a hit of hot sauce or cayenne pepper, if desired.

Check for seasoning, then ladle into soup bowls. Just before serving, sprinkle over some cheese and black pepper and serve with bread.

Cook

St Austell Tribute – UK

Moor Raw – UK

Batsmans XXXB – UK

Firestone Walker DBA – USA

Emerson's Bookbinder – New Zealand

Adnams Bitter – UK

Marble Manchester Bitter – UK

Birra Toccalmatto Stray Dog – Italy

Mordue Workie Ticket – UK

Alaskan ESB – USA

Beer-soaked Baked Cheese
Serves 2

Ingredients

1 unpasteurised Camembert or Vacherin in a wooden box

150 ml (5 fl oz/scant ⅔ cup) bourbon or whisky barrel-aged stout

1 garlic bulb, roasted

2 sprigs of thyme, leaves picked

1 teaspoon coarse sea salt

10 turns of a pepper grinder

For the accompaniments:

crusty baguette

cornichons

roasted new potatoes

celery sticks

radishes

Ok, I've said serves two here but I'm going to have to confess, it quite often serves one, because it's melted cheese and melted cheese is just so delicious.

I would like to just give you a really important piece of advice: only choose unpasteurised cheeses and do not cook it for more than 20 minutes, or it will start to harden back up and there is no rescuing it from there.

Method

A few hours before you want to bake the cheese, take it out of its wrapping, discard the plastic but keep the box.

Place the cheese in a small, non-metallic bowl and, using an oiled fork, evenly poke 5 holes, two-thirds of the depth of the cheese. Pour the beer over, return to the fridge and allow to soak in for at least an hour.

Around 10–15 minutes before you're ready to bake it, place the cheese in the freezer. This will just make it easier to cut the top off.

Whilst it's in the freezer, line the box with foil and then baking parchment. Allow these to spill over the edge, rustic is fine here.

Preheat the oven to 180°C (350°F/Gas 4).

Squeeze the roast garlic into a blender with the thyme, salt and pepper and add a tablespoon of the beer from the marinated cheese. Blend into a paste, adding more beer if necessary.

Take the cheese out of the freezer, pat dry gently with paper towels, and carefully slice the very top off, about 2 cm (1 in) down from the top. Spread the garlicky paste onto the lid of the cheese, replace it, and press down lightly. Put the cheese in the lines box.

Place in the oven for 15–20 minutes until melting and bubbly.

Serve with your chosen accompaniments and some more bourbon/whisky barrel-aged stout.

NOTE: You don't have to adhere to the garlic and herb paste idea in the method, you can use pesto or tapenade, or even forgo the paste proposition and just bake it with the beer soak and drizzle with truffled honey once it's done, the options are pretty endless.

Cook & Pair

Any of these beers will work very well as soaking beers or pairing beers.

Burning Sky Monolith – UK

Põhjala Cowboy Breakfast – Estonia

Harviestoun Ola Dubh – UK

Harvey's Imperial Stout – UK

Three Boys Imperial Oyster Stout – New Zealand

New Holland Dragon's Milk – USA

About the Author

Award-winning beer writer Melissa Cole
has spent nearly 20 years writing about the beer
and pub industry and is respected the world
over for her insight and exceptional palate.

Melissa Cole

Wandering the globe, judging
beer competitions and sharing her
business knowledge and market
experiences, has given her a unique
take on the world of beer and,
by extension, how it has grown in
stature on the dinner table.

Her knowledge of the subject is virtually unparalleled in
the UK and has seen her work with incredible restaurants
like the world-renowned St John and Michelin-starred
chefs such as Alyn Williams – not to mention with hot-
ticket events like Meatopia.

Her journey through beer and food has always been
one of shaking the norm, not accepting received wisdom
and challenging the status quo because whilst she's
renowned for many things, being quiet isn't one of them!

This book is the culmination of a personal passion
and a professional drive to get people as engaged
with cooking, and pairing, with beer as possible and, as
terrifying as she freely admits it is to put herself out there
as someone with no formal training, if she can convert
just one person, she'll be happy (for a few seconds,
before the next challenge comes along!).

Thank you

Firstly, as it always has and always will be, thank you to my tolerant and unbelievably supportive husband Ben Eaton – you are my rock, my love and my biggest cheerleader.

To my parents, Michael and Bernice Cole, you have always set me up to succeed and given me the self-belief to do so, thank you so much (and for getting Jess and Tig, so when all else fails I can come over for spaniel cuddles, they make the world so much better!).

My sister, Melanie Arnold, your constant tolerance for my demanding and nosy nature allowed me to head out in the world without fear of questioning everything... I'm sorry that you probably wince every time you hear the word 'why' now and to my brother-in-law Keith, thanks for refereeing us over the years!

My nephew Josh Arnold, you're a constant source of inspiration to me, you're a kind, smart, thoughtful young man and I'm so proud of you. My niece Kate, you are amazing, your ability to create beauty is astounding and your sass is hilarious, I love you so very much.

The Eaton clan, starting with Pam and Stan, you got me into beer and you've always stood full square behind me as I've navigated the industry, I love you both very much. Mike and Joanna Eaton, you continue to balance life and work in a way I can only aspire to and your support and love is a constant, thank you.

Jonathan Shufelt, you were one of the first people I discussed this book with and you've niggled at me about it ever since, thank you, you are a dear friend, I know you're always there.

Richard Dinwoodie and Mike Hill, I love you both, I wouldn't be where I am today without your support.

Alyn Williams, working with you over a series of events taught me so much about food, you have no idea how inspirational you are to me. To Adam Perry-Lang, Jacques Dejardin and Barbecoa, thanks for giving me my first big break in the beer and food training arena.

Meatopia massive – working with you guys is a blast and it's taught me huge amounts, same goes for the Foodies crew (and all the associated chefs and other hooligans like Charles and Catherine Metcalfe), thanks for putting up with me over the years (especially you Dhruv Baker, I can't be easy to compere but you manage to do that and be an awesome drinking buddy too!).

Joe Hurst, making sausages on the photoshoot whilst you're doing the whole 'Ghost Unchained Melody' thing in my ear was a hilarious stress release.

The rest of my industry family, all of you, I can't list you all but I am so lucky to have you in my life but I want to make special mention of some of the amazing women who have offered me love and support over the years Gwen Conley, Mirella Amato, Denise Jones, Tonya Cornett, Susanna Forbes, Annie Clements, Emma Victory and all the Crafty Beer Girls, Teri Fahrendorf, Julia Hertz, Cheryl Black, Katie Ward and so many, many more – you fabulous, feisty women all kick ass.

My friends and colleagues, who inspire and push me in my writing every day, Matthew Curtis (and Frank, of course!), Pete Brown, Adrian Tierney-Jones,

Tim Hampson, Carla Jean Lauter, Jane Peyton, Sophie Atherton, Jessica Mason and the amazing Roger Protz, thank you for being fabulous.

All the breweries that have let me through their doors over the years and all the brewers who have humoured my crazy collaboration ideas thank you, you're too numerous to mention by name here but I came away enriched from every single day.

And the organisations who continue to help me get all over the world, the Brussels Beer Challenge, the Brewer's Association, Good Beer Week, the Australian International Beer Awards, Blumenau Beer Festival, Mondiale de la Bière Diehl and the Porta Allegre festival (and of course my Brazilian family! And so many more, thank you so much for creating world-class showcases for the finest social lubricant known to man.

Special mentions must also go to James Clay, the New Zealand Beer Collective, Williams Brothers and Beer Merchants for all the beers for the photo shoots.

My friends who I just don't get to see often enough, Gillian Robson, Nicola Connors, Alberta Bussett, Miya Canty, Caroline Mair, Jamie Kenyon, Dan Fox, Bill Simmonds, Andy Martin, John Comyn, James Reader, Christine 'Booshi' Warren and so many more, forgive me!

Patricia Niven – your photos did my food more justice than I could ever have dreamed and Kathy Kordalis your skills in styling it without fakery are astonishing and your encouragement when I was having meltdowns was kindness personified. And Ollie Jarmen, for the LOLs and of course the pinch pot. And to Trev and the team at NotOnSunday for making this book look so cool, thank you so much.

To my Hardie Grant family: I really never thought this book was going to happen and you've made it a reality, Kajal, Ruth and Emma – as well as everyone else – you can't believe how much you all mean to me, you've made my dream a reality, you're all amazing women and I couldn't be luckier to have you behind me (or, even better, next to me at the bar!).

To Andrew Petrovic from Qantas for getting my iPad back to me when I left it on the plane – you're a star!

And finally, to friends old and new, new readers and long-standing supporters, thank you all, I hope you enjoy it.

Index

O

R

S

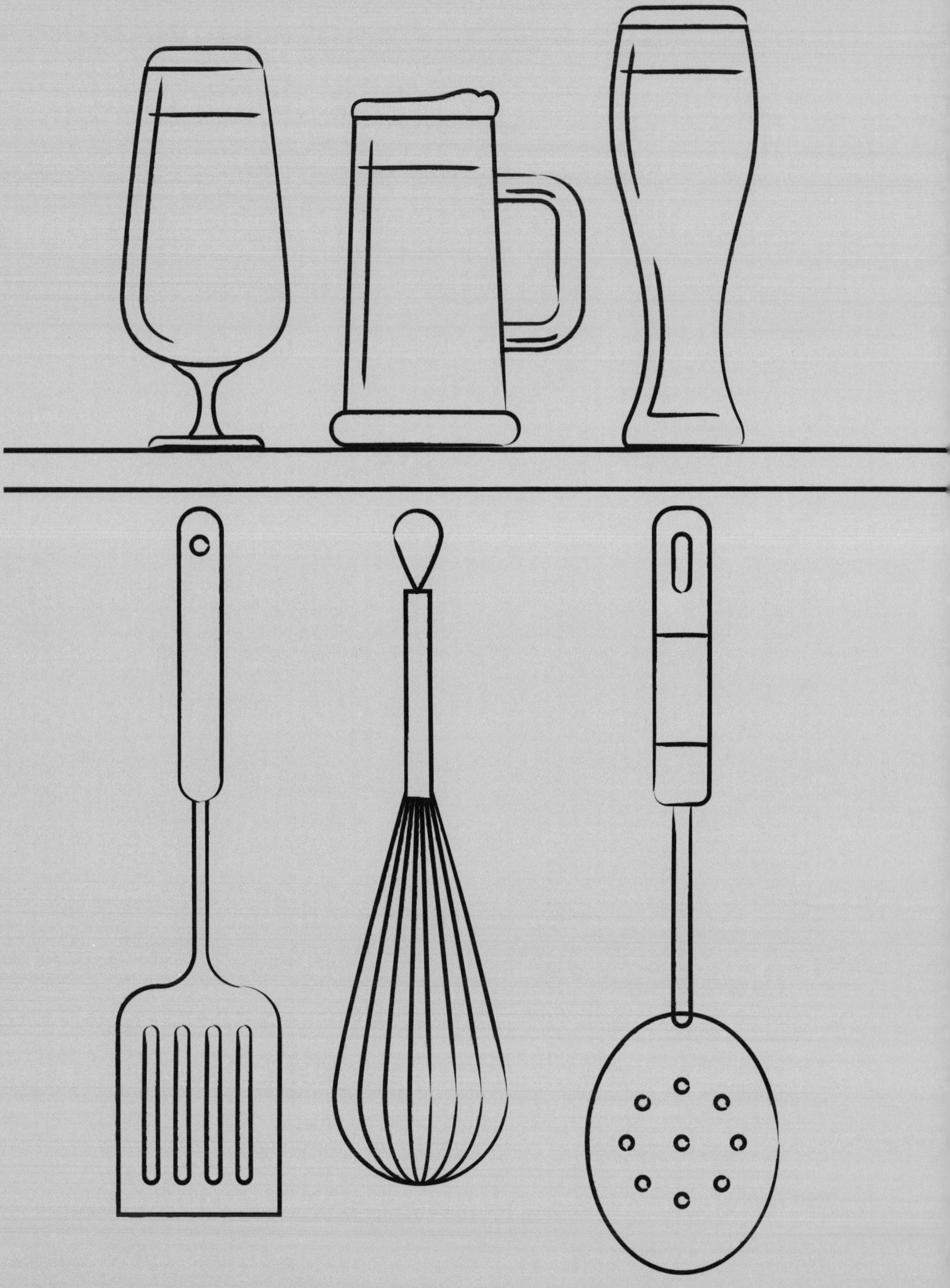

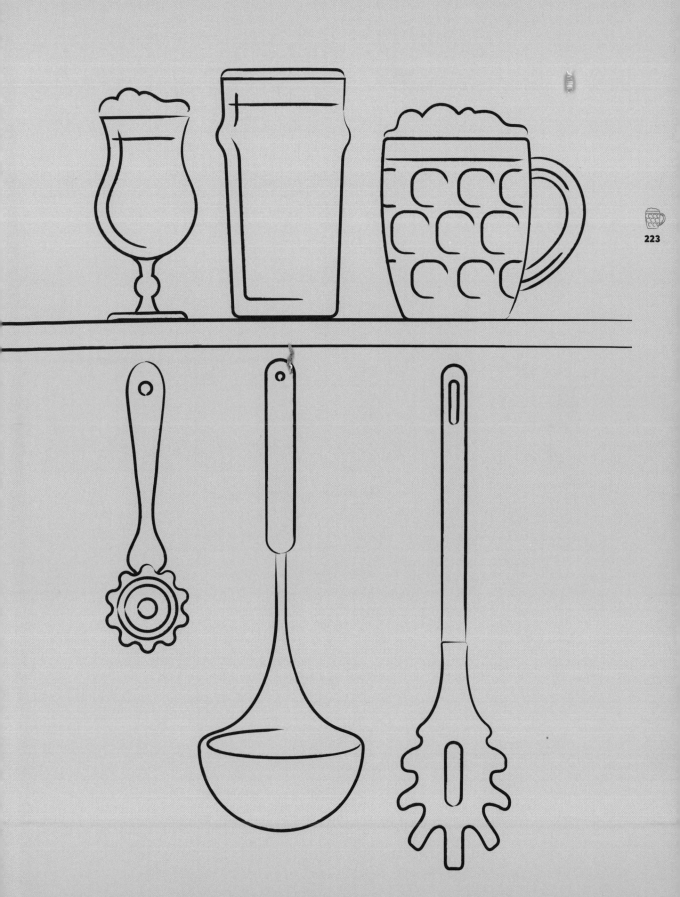

223

Published in 2018 by Hardie Grant Books, an imprint of Hardie Grant Publishing

Hardie Grant Books (London)
5th & 6th Floors
52–54 Southwark Street
London SE1 1UN

Hardie Grant Books (Melbourne)
Building 1, 658 Church Street
Richmond, Victoria 3121

hardiegrantbooks.com

British Library Cataloguing-in-Publication Data. A catalogue record for this book is available from the British Library.

The Beer Kitchen by Melissa Cole
ISBN: 978-1-78488-188-7

Publisher: Kate Pollard
Commissioning Editor: Kajal Mistry
Art Direction and Illustrations: NotOnSunday
Recipe Editor: Wendy Hobson
Proofreaders: Delphine Phin and Laura Nickoll
Photographer: Patricia Niven
Photography Assistant: Ollie Jarman
Author Photo on page 206 © Steve Ryan
Food Stylist: Kathy Kordalis
Food Stylist Assistants: Anna Hiddleston and Rebecca Spooner
Prop Stylist: Ginger Whisk
Indexer: Cathy Heath

Colour Reproduction by p2d
Printed and bound in China by Leo Paper Group

[1] https://www.skepticalraptor.com/skepticalraptorblog.php/msg-myth-versus-science/
[2] https://www.sciencedirect.com/science/article/pii/S0950329310001217